Foreword
はじめに

It is with great pleasure that I bring forth this second volume of "Surprising Japan," a textbook based on my columns in *The Japan Times*. I have been so gratified that the first volume, which was published by Shohakusha in 2012, has been in constant use ever since in university classrooms all over Japan. Like my newspaper column, the me was based on real questions posed by non-Japanese people  pan but don't understand. For this second volume, I have ad for Japanese students of English. It is my hope that the essays elp students see Japan with fresh eyes, and provide them with y need to go forth to share the wonders of their own country a world.

Alice Gordenker, Tokyo 2016

The Japan Times 掲載の私のコラムをもとにした *Surprising Japan!* の第2作目をご紹介できることをとても嬉しく思っています。*Surprising Japan!* は、2012年の刊行以降、全国の大学のクラスで継続的にご採用頂いています。新聞でのコラムと同様、この第1作目は、日本で目にしながらも理解できない事柄について海外の人たちから実際に寄せられた質問に基づいたものでした。今回は本書のために、15の新しいエッセイを英語を学ぶ日本の学生向けに改作いたしました。本書のエッセイや練習問題が、学生に日本を違った角度で見る視点を与え、自国の素晴らしさ、そしてその文化を世界と共有するために必要な洞察力と語彙を提供できればこれ以上ありません。

アリス・ゴーデンカー
2016年東京にて

I have very much enjoyed using "Surprising Japan" with my university students, as it has given them the opportunity to consider aspects of Japanese culture that they may have taken for granted. By reading about actual questions asked by people from other countries, Japanese students can go beyond stereotypical ideas like "Japan is unique because it has the four seasons" and learn more about their own culture while also learning English. I'm very excited about the continued great range of topics in this second volume. There is something of interest for everyone, from everyday topics like Japanese cuisine to social issues like organ donation. My hope is that Japanese university students will use this book to both develop their ability to describe their own culture in English and consider what it means to be Japanese in a rapidly globalizing world.

John Rucynski, Kobe 2016

私は大学で学生と *Surprising Japan!* を非常に楽しんで使っています。彼らが当たり前と思っている日本の文化の捉え方を考え直す機会を提供しているからです。他国の人からの実際の質問を読み知ることにより、日本の学生は、たとえば「日本は四季があるから特異である」といった型通りの考え方を超越でき、さらに英語を学びながら同時に自国の文化についてより多く学ぶことができるのです。本書においても前作から引き継がれている幅広いトピックに心躍る思いです。本書は日本食といった日常的なものから臓器提供などの社会問題にいたるまで、すべての人にとって興味をひく事柄を扱っております。日本の学生に、自らの文化を英語で表現する能力を身につけさせるだけでなく、急速にグローバル化する世界において、日本人であることの意味を考えることができるようになるために、この教科書を使って頂けることを願っています。

ジョン・ルシンスキ
2016年神戸にて

Surprising Japan! 2

Contents

Chapter 1

What makes Kobe beef so special?

高級牛肉

次の質問について考えてみましょう。

1. What is the best food you have eaten recently? What made it so good? What are the special features of this food?

2. What food would you like to eat for a special occasion, such as your birthday? For example, would you like to eat a very expensive food or a cheap and simple food?

Vocabulary Check

🔊 Audio 01

次の単語の意味を a〜i のなかから選びましょう。

1. _____ competition (*n.*)
2. _____ prefecture (*n.*)
3. _____ cattle (*n.*)
4. _____ resident (*n.*)
5. _____ high-quality (*adj.*)
6. _____ spread (*v.*)
7. _____ melt (*v.*)
8. _____ certified (*adj.*)
9. _____ protect (*v.*)

a. an administrative division of Japan, such as Hyogo and Mie
b. animals used for meat or milk
c. move from place to place; become bigger or more popular
d. a person who lives in a particular place
e. a situation where there are many different products or brands to choose from
f. become softer; change from a solid to a liquid
g. keep from harm or damage
h. very good; well-made or well-designed
i. proven or guaranteed

Pre-reading Quiz

本文を読む前に次の質問について答えましょう。

What are the three most famous brands of beef in Japan?

1. *Kobe beef (Hyogo Prefecture)*

2. _____

3. _____

Reading

An American on his first visit to Japan wants to try Kobe beef. He's heard it's the most delicious meat in the world.

My first question when I arrived in Japan was, "Where can I get Kobe beef?" I've wanted to try Kobe beef ever since I first heard about it many years ago. I've heard that the cows are fed beer, listen to classical music, and get daily massages. People say that Kobe beef is the best beef in the world. I was really surprised
5 when my Japanese friend told me that Kobe beef has competition. He told me it is only one of several famous brands of beef in Japan. Other premium brands include Matsuzaka beef from Mie Prefecture and Omi beef from Shiga Prefecture.

So why is only Kobe beef internationally famous? My friend explained that
10 when Yokohama first opened to foreign trade in 1859, foreigners couldn't buy beef. In Japan, cattle were kept only as work animals and not for meat. Foreign residents learned that high-quality cattle were raised in the western part of the country, in a place called Tajima. So, they arranged to buy some and bring it to Yokohama by boat. The port closest to the cattle farms was Kobe, so foreigners
15 began to call the meat "Kobe beef." When they returned to their countries, they told stories about the delicious beef they ate in Japan. The fame of Kobe beef spread.

What exactly makes Tajima cattle so special? Tajima cows have fine muscle fiber and a high degree of fat marbling. In addition, the fat has a low melting
20 point so it seems to melt in your mouth. But only the best meat from Tajima cows can be certified as Kobe beef. The animals do require special care, but it turns out the stories about music, massage and beer just aren't true. The continued high quality is because farmers have protected the pure Tajima bloodline for hundreds of years.

25 Guess what I'm having for dinner tonight: yes, Kobe beef!

 314 words

NOTES
l. 18-19: muscle fiber 筋線維　l. 19: marbling (肉の) 霜降り、さし　l. 21: certify (物・事) を保証する　l. 23: bloodline (動物・人間の) 血統

Reading Comprehension: True or False

本文で述べられていることについて正しいものに T、間違っているものに F を選び○で囲みましょう。

1. (T　F)　Several types of Japanese beef are internationally famous.
2. (T　F)　The first people to eat Kobe beef were foreign residents of Japan.
3. (T　F)　Kobe beef tastes better because the cows are given beer and massages.

Listening: Dialogue

📶 Audio 03

次の会話を聴き、空所を埋めましょう。

Alice and John are talking about what to eat for dinner.

Alice: Are you hungry? Let's get something to eat.

John: Yeah, I'm starving! What do you ① _____ _____ _____?

Alice: I'm really ② _____ _____ _____ for Kobe beef.

John: Kobe beef again? We just had it last week. We can't ③ _____ Kobe beef again. It's too expensive.

Alice: Yes, I know it's expensive, but it's ④ _____ _____. It's the best beef in the world!

John: Sure, it tastes great, but the ⑤ _____ are too small. Let's go for a big, ⑥ _____ bowl of ramen instead. It's a much better value.

Alice: Don't worry about price. Dinner's on me! I think ⑦ _____ is more important than ⑧ _____.

John: OK! As long as you're ⑨ _____, I'm in the mood for Kobe beef too.

True or False

もう一度会話を聴き、正しいものに T を、間違っているものに F を○で囲みましょう。

1. (T F) At first, John wants to eat Kobe beef.

2. (T F) Alice thinks it's fine to spend a lot of money for a meal.

3. (T F) Alice will pay for John's dinner.

Grammar Check

会話に出てきた表現を確認しながら（　　　）内の適切な語を選びましょう。

1. What (ⓐ are ⓑ do) you feel like doing tonight?

2. I'm (ⓐ in ⓑ on) the mood for pizza.

3. I paid 10,000 yen for this shirt, but it was (ⓐ worth ⓑ worthy) it.

4. Let's have fruit for dessert instead (ⓐ to ⓑ of) ice cream. I'm on a diet.

Discussion Questions

パートナーと次のトピックについて話し合ってみましょう。

1. Some people believe spending a lot of money on one meal is worth it. Other people, however, think it's a waste of money. What's your opinion? How much money do you think it's OK to spend on one meal? Why?

2. Kobe beef is internationally famous, but there are so many other wonderful Japanese foods. Imagine that someone from another country is coming to dinner at your home. What Japanese dishes would you like to prepare for them? Why?

高級牛肉

The top three most famous brands of Japanese beef are Kobe beef (Hyogo), Matsuzaka beef (Mie) and Omi beef (Shiga). Here are some other famous top-three rankings. Fill in the blanks with the numbers from the map and write the answers in the parentheses.

Three Great Views (of Japan)

1. __4__ (*Matsushima*)

2. _____ ( )

3. _____ ( )

Three Famous Gardens

1. _____ ( )

2. _____ ( )

3. _____ ( )

Three Great Castles

1. _____ ( )

2. _____ ( )

3. _____ ( )

Three Great Festivals

1. _____ ( )

2. _____ ( )

3. _____ ( )

Chapter 2

What are those backpacks Japanese schoolchildren wear?

ランドセル

Warm-up Questions

次の質問について考えてみましょう。

1. Can you remember getting your first backpack (ランドセル) when you were an elementary school student? What color was it? Were you excited to get it?

2. What is your best memory from your elementary school days? What moment or event was most special for you?

Vocabulary Check

🔊 Audio 04

次の単語の意味を a〜i のなかから選びましょう。

1. _____ purchase (v.)
2. _____ expectation (n.)
3. _____ last (v.)
4. _____ range (n.)
5. _____ similar (adj.)
6. _____ compartment (n.)
7. _____ affluent (adj.)
8. _____ preference (n.)
9. _____ market (n.)

a. almost the same as something else
b. continue for a long time; stay in good condition
c. a part or space of something
d. rich or wealthy
e. hope; desire; wish
f. a way or place of selling and buying goods
g. liking one thing more than another
h. buy or get
i. variety of styles, prices, designs, etc.

Pre-reading Quiz

本文を読む前に次の質問について答えましょう。

The word *randoseru* comes from which language?

a) German   **b)** Dutch   **c)** Portuguese

Reading

A Canadian mother visiting Japan is curious about the box-like backpacks that Japanese schoolchildren wear.

The backpacks used by schoolchildren in Japan are called *randoseru*, which comes from the Dutch word *ransel*. Families purchase a new *randoseru* when a child enters school at the age of six, with the expectation that the child will use it for all six years of primary school. Accordingly, *randoseru* are built to last. Prices
5 range from 20,000 to 100,000 yen or more, with many families paying around 50,000 yen.

Despite this range in prices, *randoseru* are surprisingly similar. They all have two back-straps attached to an upright rectangle that is divided into two main compartments — a large one for books and a smaller one for papers and pencil
10 case. The top is covered by a long flap that comes over the compartments and closes on the front. This is called the "Gakushuin style," after the prestigious Tokyo school that first introduced them in 1885. Other private schools followed Gakushuin's example, but *randoseru* were rare outside of big cities.

Most children carried their books to school in a *furoshiki* cloth wrapper. But
15 in the early 1960s, as families became more affluent, *randoseru* became a "must have" item for schoolchildren. Boys generally had black *randoseru*; girls almost always used red ones. No one is sure how these color preferences developed, but one theory is that they came from *geta*, the traditional wooden clogs that children used to wear. In the early postwar period, when *randoseru* became popular, the
20 straps on children's *geta* were usually black for boys and red for girls. Today, children can choose *randoseru* in a much wider selection of colors. Black is still popular with boys, but blue, brown and green are gaining market share. Girls now prefer pink over red. And when purple was introduced in 2010, it immediately grabbed eight percent of the market for girls.

300 words

ⓃⓄⓉⒺⓈ ||||||||||||||||||||||||||||||||||||||||||||||||||||||||||||||||||||||||||||||||||||||||||||||||

l. 10: flap（ポケットなどについた）平たい垂れぶた　l. 11: prestigious 有名な　l. 15: affluent 裕福な　l. 20: strap (of a *geta*) 鼻緒

Reading Comprehension: True or False

本文で述べられていることについて正しいものに T、間違っているものに F を選び○で囲みましょう。

1. (T F) Makers of *randoseru* expect that children need a new one every few years.

2. (T F) *Randoseru* are made in a wide range of designs.

3. (T F) As Japan became a richer nation, *randoseru* became more common.

ランドセル

Listening: Dialogue

🔊 Audio 06

次の会話を聴き、空所を埋めましょう。

Peter asks Mari about the big backpacks he sees elementary school children carrying.

Peter: Wow, what's up with that backpack? It's ①_____ _____ _____ that little boy is.

Mari: What are you ②_____ _____?

Peter: Over there. That little boy is carrying a giant backpack. It's really cute, but it looks too ③_____ _____ _____.

Mari: Oh that. You mean a *randoseru*. All Japanese elementary school children ④_____ _____ _____ them.

Peter: So they need both a uniform and a backpack? But the school ⑤_____ them, right?

Mari: No, of course not. Parents or grandparents ⑥_____ _____ _____ for the children.

Peter: But do they need a new one every year? They look quite ⑦_____-_____ and expensive.

Mari: No, the idea is they should use the same one throughout their ⑧_____ _____ in elementary school.

Peter: Ah, that makes sense. They look like they're ⑨_____ _____ _____.

True or False

もう一度会話を聴き、正しいものにTを、間違っているものにFを〇で囲みましょう。

1. (T F) Peter thinks the backpack is the proper size for the child he sees.

2. (T F) Peter guesses that *randoseru* are paid for by the school.

3. (T F) Peter imagines *randoseru* probably last for a long time.

Grammar Check

会話に出てきた表現を確認しながら（　　　）内の適切な語を選びましょう。

1. My new house is twice (ⓐ bigger than ⓑ as big as) my old house.

2. If you want to watch the game, you (ⓐ have ⓑ has) to have a ticket.

3. I'm so hungry, I could eat a (ⓐ all ⓑ whole) pizza by myself.

4. I've already spent (ⓐ all ⓑ whole) of my money, so I can't go to dinner tonight.

Discussion Questions

パートナーと次のトピックについて話し合ってみましょう。

1. In Japan, a *randoseru* is basically required equipment for elementary school children, and almost everyone uses nearly the exact same style. How do you feel about this?

2. In some countries, including Japan, students wear uniforms to school. In other countries, however, students are free to wear whatever they like. Which system do you think is better? Give reasons to support your opinion.

Read the clues and fill in the correct answers from the list of words provided.

School

(club   fail   notebook   exam   chalkboard   backpack   absent   major
president   principal   homework   cafeteria   pass   pencil)

Across

6. your main area of study at university
7. something you study hard for
9. something the teacher writes on
11. what you carry your books in
12. what you write with in class
13. a group you do an activity with before or after school
14. what you are if you don't go to class

Down

1. the place where students eat lunch
2. something lazy students hate
3. what you take notes in
4. to successfully complete a class
5. the head of a school
8. the head of a university
10. to not get a good enough score to pass a class

Chapter 3

What are the seven things in *shichimi*?

七味

Warm-up Questions

次の質問について考えてみましょう。

1. Do you like spicy food? If so, what kinds of spicy food do you usually eat?

2. When you eat in a restaurant, do you like to eat the food as it is served? Or do you like to add some toppings or seasoning? What do you like to add to your food?

Vocabulary Check

🔊 **Audio 07**

次の単語の意味を a ～ i のなかから選びましょう。

1. _____ curious (*adj.*)
2. _____ jar (*n.*)
3. _____ seasoning (*n.*)
4. _____ frequently (*adv.*)
5. _____ sprinkle (*v.*)
6. _____ heat (*n.*)
7. _____ familiar (*adj.*)
8. _____ contain (*v.*)
9. _____ substitute (*v.*)

a. herbs or spices, such as salt and pepper, which are added to food to give it more flavor
b. have or hold something in it
c. spicy taste in a food
d. change one thing for another
e. happen or do often
f. interested in something; want to know or learn more
g. add some topping to a food; usually in small amounts
h. know about or have experience with
i. a container for holding food or other small objects

Pre-reading Quiz

本文を読む前に次の質問について答えましょう。

As you'd expect from the name, there are (usually) seven ingredients in *shichimi*. How many of them can you name?

A student from Peru wants to know about the spice blend he sees on tables in restaurants and cafeterias in Japan.

I love spicy food. That's why I became so curious about the little jars of red spice I often see in restaurants and the cafeteria at my university in Japan. My Japanese friends told me it's called *shichimi*, which means "seven flavors," but no one could tell me what the seven flavors are. So I decided to find out for myself.

5 I did some research in the library and stores, and learned that *shichimi* is a very popular seasoning in Japan. Almost every home in Japan has *shichimi* in the kitchen, and many restaurants keep it on the table so customers can add it as they wish. It is frequently enjoyed with noodle dishes such as soba and udon. Many people sprinkle it on other foods, including yakitori and *gyūdon* (flavored beef on 10 rice). It's also delicious on *unagi* (grilled eel). The ingredient that gives *shichimi* its heat is *tōgarashi*, which is capsicum, a type of chili pepper. I'm of course familiar with capsicum, because it's native to South America. Chili pepper is used in lots of Peruvian dishes.

For the last part of my research, I visited a shop in Tokyo's Asakusa district 15 that is famous for *shichimi*. It's called Yagenbori. They've been making *shichimi* for almost 400 years. Originally, during the Edo period, *shichimi* was sold as a medicine, because the ingredients are good for your health. Yagenbori's original *chūkara* (medium-spicy) blend contains the following seven ingredients: black sesame seeds, dried capsicum, roasted dry capsicum, the dried peel of the *unshu* 20 *mikan* (Satsuma orange), *sanshō* (Japanese pepper), poppy seeds and hemp seeds. Other companies sometimes substitute one or more of these ingredients for other spices, such as ginger or seaweed, and some blends don't have exactly seven ingredients. One contained *eight*! What kind of a seven-flavor spice is *that*?

🖊 301 words

NOTES
l. 7: so ～するように、～するために   l. 10: ingredient 原料   l. 11: capsicum トウガラシ   l. 13: Peruvian ペルーの

Reading Comprehension: True or False

本文で述べられていることについて正しいものに T、間違っているものに F を選び○で囲みましょう。

1. (T F) Most Japanese people can name all the ingredients in *shichimi*.
2. (T F) A long time ago, *shichimi* was sold as a medicine.
3. (T F) *Shichimi* always contains seven ingredients.

Listening: Dialogue

Audio 09 七味

次の会話を聴き、空所を埋めましょう。

Koji and Susan are enjoying sushi together.

Koji: Wow, that's a lot of wasabi. Why are you putting so much wasabi on your sushi?

Susan: Hey, I like wasabi. What's ① _____ _____ _____ ?

Koji: Actually, you only need a ② _____ _____ to add flavor. That's the ③ _____ way to eat sushi.

Susan: But I like very ④ _____ _____ and the kick from wasabi.

Koji: But the ⑤ _____ of the flavors is most important. And some types of fish don't need any wasabi ⑥ _____ _____ .

Susan: Hey, you eat sushi ⑦ _____ _____ and I'll eat sushi ⑧ _____ _____ .

Koji: Haven't you heard the expression "When in ⑨ _____ , do as the ⑩ _____ do"? By the way, would you like some more beer?

Susan: No, thanks. I think it's ⑪ _____ to drink sake with sushi.

True or False

もう一度会話を聴き、正しいものにTを、間違っているものにFを○で囲みましょう。

1. (T F) Susan likes putting a lot of wasabi on her sushi.

2. (T F) Susan and Koji agree about the best way to eat sushi.

3. (T F) Susan and Koji agree about what to drink with sushi.

Grammar Check

会話に出てきた表現を確認しながら（　　　）内の適切な語を選びましょう。

1. I like to (ⓐ put ⓑ putting) a lot of ketchup on French fries.

2. I like (ⓐ put ⓑ putting) *shichimi* on yakitori.

3. I need (ⓐ many ⓑ a lot of) money to buy a new car.

4. I went shopping all day, so I don't have any money (ⓐ at ⓑ of) all.

Discussion Questions

パートナーと次のトピックについて話し合ってみましょう。

1. If you were going to study abroad or live in a foreign country, which Japanese foods or seasonings do you think you would miss the most? Why?

2. Imagine you were going on a long camping trip and you could only bring one seasoning or spice with you to flavor your food. Which one would you bring? Why? Name some of the different foods you could season with this spice.

What's in the Japanese kitchen?

You can find many interesting condiments, seasonings, and spices in the typical Japanese kitchen. Match each word on the left with the correct description on the right.

1. _____ *dashi*

2. _____ *furikake*

3. _____ ginger

4. _____ *karashi*

5. _____ *mirin*

6. _____ miso

7. _____ *ponzu*

8. _____ *sanshō*

9. _____ wasabi

10. _____ *yuzu*

a. fermented soybeans, often used for making soup

b. a spicy green paste often called Japanese horseradish

c. a spicy mustard used in dipping sauces or on Chinese dumplings

d. a citrus fruit used to season some foods and also used in some alcoholic drinks

e. a plant used to season dishes or served pickled with sushi

f. a dry seasoning most frequently sprinkled on rice to give it flavor

g. a rice wine used in cooking, usually with sugar and soy sauce

h. a sauce made by combining citrus juice with soy sauce

i. a kind of Japanese pepper with a very strong taste

j. broth made from fish flakes and other ingredients; used as the base for miso soup and many traditional Japanese dishes

Chapter 4

Why does Japan's postal symbol look like that?

〒 マーク

次の質問について考えてみましょう。

1. What do you think Japan's postal symbol (〒) means? Why was this symbol chosen?

2. Do you think this symbol is used in other countries too? Or is it unique to Japan? Why? Share your opinion with your partner.

Vocabulary Check

🔊 Audio 10

次の単語の意味を a 〜 j のなかから選びましょう。

1. _____ assume (*v.*)	**a.** true or the same all over the world
2. _____ warn (*v.*)	**b.** bring something to someone
3. _____ recognized (*adj.*)	**c.** a person who brings or carries mail or packages
4. _____ deliver (*v.*)	**d.** keep in a place for future use
5. _____ approximately (*adv.*)	**e.** permanently placed somewhere
6. _____ courier (*n.*)	**f.** advise someone to be careful
7. _____ fixed (*adj.*)	**g.** close to; almost the same as
8. _____ store (*v.*)	**h.** believe something is true without truth or facts
9. _____ advocate (*v.*)	**i.** support; be in favor of
10. _____ universal (*adj.*)	**j.** known by many people

Pre-reading Quiz

本文を読む前に次の質問について答えましょう。

When was Japan's postal symbol created?

a) 1603 **b)** 1887 **c)** 1923

Reading

A Swedish student wants to know about the Japanese postal mark, which he has never seen before. In Sweden, and many other European countries, the symbol for the postal system is a horn.

Many Japanese assume the symbol for their postal system is used all over the world, but actually, it's used only in Japan. In fact, the Japan Post website warns that Japan's postal symbol should not be written on mail going to other countries because it won't be understood. But within Japan this mark, which looks like the

5 letter "T" with a bar over the top, is widely recognized as the symbol for the post system. It was designed in 1887 for the newly created Ministry of Communications and Transportation (Teishin-shō), which was given the responsibility for developing a modern postal system. The symbol is based on the katakana *te* for *teishin*.

10 Japan's first official system for delivering messages was organized in the seventh century. Based on a model in China, it consisted of a series of postal stations (called *eki*, the same word we use today for train stations). Each station was spaced approximately 16 kilometers apart. Couriers relayed messages from one station to the next, along a fixed line. By the middle of the 19th century,

15 there were both public and private delivery services, all based on this station system. The couriers who ran between the stations came to be known as *hikyaku*, which literally means "flying legs." They ran their routes in pairs, with the mail safely stored in a wooden box on the end of a pole they carried over their shoulders.

20 Hisoka Maejima (1835-1919) was a statesman, politician and businessman who created the modern Japanese postal service. He advocated low-cost, universal service and the use of prepaid postal stamps. Maejima personally coined the Japanese words for "post" (*yūbin*), "stamp" (*kitte*), and "postcard" (*hagaki*), and is known as "Yūbin Seido no Chichi" ("Father of the Postal System"). You can see

25 his face on the 1-yen stamp.

✏ 299 words

NOTES ‖‖‖
l. 13: relay 伝える　courier ＝messenger　l. 14: line 路線　l. 17: route 配達区域　in pairs 二人一組で
l. 20: statesman 立派な指導者、政治屋　l. 21: advocate 主張する　l. 22: coin （新語などを）造り出す

Reading Comprehension: True or False

本文で述べられていることについて正しいものに T、間違っているものに F を選び○で囲みましょう。

1. (T　F)　Japan Post advises people to write the postal symbol on all mail.

2. (T　F)　Japan's postal system is more than one hundred years old.

3. (T　F)　Hisoka Maejima created the postal system especially for rich people.

Listening: Dialogue

🔊 Audio 12

〒
マ
ー
ク

次の会話を聴き、空所を埋めましょう。

Amanda and Kenji are talking about Japan's postal system.

Amanda: Japan's postal system is really amazing, isn't it?

Kenji: What ① _____ _____ say that? What's so ② _____ about Japan's postal system?

Amanda: I'm talking about the New Year's ③ _____. It's amazing that people send ④ _____ of cards each year, but they all arrive on time!

Kenji: Well, to ⑤ _____ the _____, I don't send so many New Year's cards anymore.

Amanda: Oh, why not? It's such a ⑥ _____ _____ and the cards are beautifully decorated.

Kenji: Yeah, but it's such a ⑦ _____ to write so many by hand. I send most of my New Year's greetings by ⑧ _____ or e-mail now.

Amanda: Oh, that's a ⑨ _____. I think writing cards by hand shows more consideration. After all, it's the thought that counts.

Kenji: I ⑩ _____ _____ _____. So, I promise to send you a hand-written card this year!

True or False

もう一度会話を聴き、正しいものに T を、間違っているものに F を◯で囲みましょう。

1. (T F) Kenji agrees with Amanda that Japan's postal system is amazing.
2. (T F) Kenji thinks writing New Year's cards by hand is better.
3. (T F) In the end, Kenji understands Amanda's opinion about New Year's cards.

Grammar Check

会話に出てきた表現を確認しながら （　　　）内の適切な語を選びましょう。

1. There's a lot of great food in Hokkaido, (ⓐ isn't it? ⓑ isn't there?)
2. That director makes a lot of great movies, (ⓐ don't he? ⓑ doesn't he?)
3. I like to send (ⓐ many ⓑ much) Christmas cards every year.
4. I spend (ⓐ almost ⓑ most) of my free time reading.

Discussion Questions

パートナーと次のトピックについて話し合ってみましょう。

1. Do you usually write traditional New Year's cards or do you send New Year's greetings electronically? Which way do you think is better? Why?
2. Imagine that a person from another country has asked you to how to write a Japanese New Year's card. What advice would you give? Are there any rules or customs they should know?

Read the clues and fill in the correct answers from the list of words provided.

Post Office

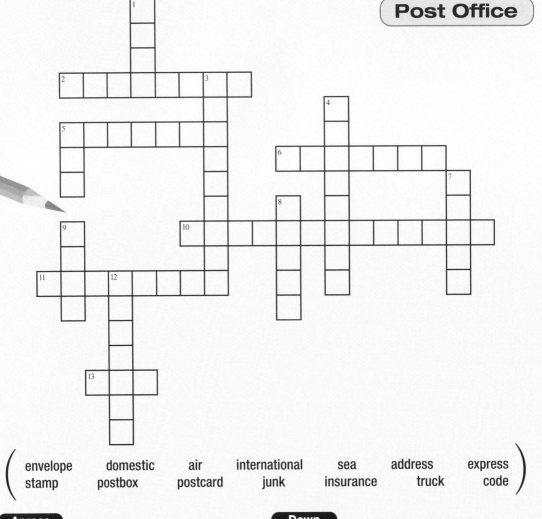

envelope   domestic   air   international   sea   address   express
stamp   postbox   postcard   junk   insurance   truck   code

Across

2. mail sent within your own country is called _____ mail
5. the location of the person you are sending mail to
6. you can put your mail in here instead of going to the post office
10. mail sent to other countries is called _____ mail
11. you put a letter or card in this before mailing it
13. mail delivered by ship is called _____ mail

Down

1. the numbers at the end of an address are called the zip _____
3. what you pay in case something happens to your package
4. what many Japanese send to arrive on New Year's Day
5. mail delivered by plane is called _____ mail
7. something you need to attach to letters or postcards before sending them
8. post office workers deliver bigger mail in this vehicle
9. mail no one wants to get (such as catalogues) is called _____ mail
12. mail which you pay extra for to arrive more quickly is called _____ mail

Chapter 5

Why is there plastic grass in my bento?

Warm-up Questions

次の質問について考えてみましょう。

1. How often do you eat bento? What are your favorite kinds of bento?

2. Many bento come with small pieces of green plastic that look like grass. Why do you think they are there? Discuss with your partner and try to guess the reasons.

Vocabulary Check

🔊 **Audio 13**

次の単語の意味を a 〜 j のなかから選びましょう。

1. _____ attractive (*adj.*)
2. _____ decoration (*n.*)
3. _____ separate (*v.*)
4. _____ transfer (*v.*)
5. _____ prepared (*adj.*)
6. _____ leaf (*n.*)
7. _____ wealthy (*adj.*)
8. _____ excursion (*n.*)
9. _____ rot (*v.*)
10. _____ bacteria (*n.*)

a. rich; has a lot of money
b. ready; already made by someone
c. move from one place to another
d. divide; keep different objects from touching each other
e. microorganisms that cause sickness or disease
f. become old; go bad
g. a short trip or journey
h. looks good; pleasing to the eye
i. an object that makes something look nicer, such as a Christmas ornament
j. a green part that grows on a plant and falls from a tree

Pre-reading Quiz

本文を読む前に次の質問について答えましょう。

In what era was the bento originally developed?

a) Edo period **b)** Meiji period **c)** Showa period

Reading

A young Argentine visiting Japan on a high-school exchange program wants to know why there is plastic "grass" in her bento box lunch. Her Japanese host sister explains.

Those pieces of green plastic, cut on one end so they do look a little like grass, are called *haran* (sometimes *baran*). They make the bento look more attractive by adding color, but they aren't just for decoration. Their most important function is to separate foods. In bento making, several types of dividers are used to keep
5 foods from touching. This prevents strong flavors from transferring from one food to another. Keeping foods separate also slows bacterial growth, so the bento will stay fresh and safe to eat for a longer period of time.

Japanese people have long had simple ways to carry prepared foods away from home, such as wrapping cooked rice in leaves to be eaten later while working
10 in the fields. But the bento as we know it — small amounts of many foods packed together in a beautiful box — developed during the Edo period. In those days, wealthy people ordered special meals for outdoor parties and excursions. The food needed to be packed tightly to prevent it from moving around during transport, but it also had to look good because playful, attractive presentations
15 were prized.

Originally, real leaves were used to separate the foods in bento. Some plants, when their leaves are damaged, release antimicrobial substances called phytoncides that prevent the leaf from rotting. When such leaves are used to wrap or divide foods, these substances slow the growth of bacteria. Plastic
20 substitutes were introduced in the mid-1960s, when supermarkets first started appearing in Japan. The big stores were looking for ways to cut costs so they could offer lower prices. Plastic dividers are cheaper than real leaves, and save labor because they don't require special handling. In recent years, with the internationalization of sushi, the plastic variety has spread overseas, where it is
25 sold as "sushi grass."

🖊 301 words

ＮＯＴＥＳ ||||||||||||||||||||||||||||||||||||||||||||||||||||||||||||||||||||||||||||||||||||||||||||||||||||||||||||||||||||||||||

Argentine アルゼンチン人　l. 9: leaves　leaf の複数形　l. 14: playful 遊び心のある　l. 15: prize ～を高く評価する
l. 17: release ～を放出する　antimicrobial 抗菌性の　l. 18: rot 腐る　l. 20: substitute 代用品　l. 23: handling 処理

Reading Comprehension: True or False

本文で述べられていることについて正しいものに T、間違っているものに F を選び○で囲みましょう。

1. (T F) The main function of *haran* is to make the bento more attractive.
2. (T F) Bento were originally developed for rich people.
3. (T F) Before plastic dividers were invented, people used real leaves when making bento.

Listening: Dialogue

次の会話を聴き、空所を埋めましょう。

Takuya explains bento grass to his home-stay sister, Sofia.

Sofia: Hey, what's this in my bento? Is that ① _____ ?

Takuya: Don't worry about it. It's not ② _____ _____ . It's just a plastic divider.

Sofia: But what's it there for? Is it just for decoration? What a ③ _____ !

Takuya: Many people ④ _____ it's for decoration, but actually the ⑤ _____ _____ is to separate different foods.

Sofia: But why do you ⑥ _____ _____ _____ about separating the food? It all goes in the same ⑦ _____ .

Takuya: It's not just about the taste. The most important thing is to stop bacteria ⑧ _____ _____ .

Sofia: I didn't realize that. That's quite ⑨ _____ ! Now I get it.

Takuya: Yeah, and if you can slow the growth of bacteria, the bento will stay ⑩ _____ _____ .

Sofia: Well, I guess you ⑪ _____ _____ _____ every day!

True or False

もう一度会話を聴き、正しいものに T を、間違っているものに F を○で囲みましょう。

1. (T F)　Sofia is surprised to find something like grass in her bento.

2. (T F)　Many people think bento grass is just for decoration.

3. (T F)　In the end, Sofia thinks bento grass is a good idea.

Grammar Check

会話に出てきた表現を確認しながら (　　　) 内の適切な語を選びましょう。

1. The main purpose of bento grass is to (ⓐ separate ⓑ separation) different foods.

2. (ⓐ Dividing ⓑ Division) different foods keeps bacteria from growing.

3. November is too early to start (ⓐ decorate ⓑ decorating) the Christmas tree.

4. Could you please explain it again? I just don't (ⓐ get ⓑ got) it.

Discussion Questions

パートナーと次のトピックについて話し合ってみましょう。

1. Some people believe that bento are good for you, while others claim they are just a kind of fast food. What's your opinion? Is a bento a healthy food choice? Give reasons to support your opinion.

2. A recent trend is to make bento with cute designs, such as rice balls decorated to look like a panda or soccer ball. How do you feel about such cute food? If you have children in the future, would you spend extra time to make their bento cute?

Ekiben

Japanese people love ekiben, *special bento sold at train stations all over Japan. How many famous* ekiben *do you know? Match the* ekiben *description on the right with the prefecture where it is most famous.*

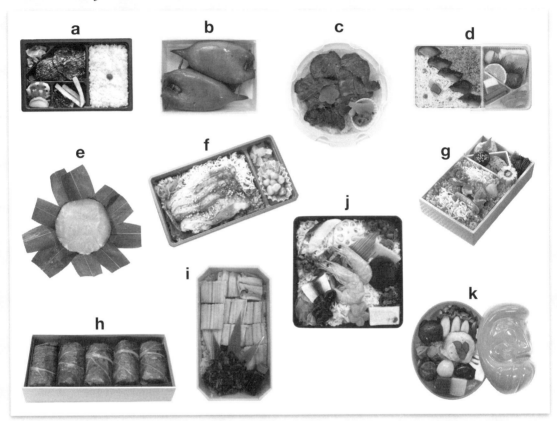

1. _____ Akita	**a.**	features one of the best brands of beef in Japan
2. _____ Gunma	**b.**	features squid stuffed with rice
3. _____ Hiroshima	**c.**	topped with thinly-sliced pieces of beef tongue
4. _____ Hokkaido	**d.**	chicken with sliced *shiitake* mushrooms and fried egg
5. _____ Mie	**e.**	rice topped with slices of salmon trout in a disk-shaped box
6. _____ Miyagi	**f.**	delicious Awa chicken with sliced fried egg over tea-flavored rice
7. _____ Miyazaki	**g.**	soy sauce-flavored chicken served over seasoned rice
8. _____ Okayama	**h.**	rice balls packed in pickled mustard leaves
9. _____ Tokushima	**i.**	grilled eel served over rice; sold in one of the three most scenic spots in Japan
10. _____ Toyama	**j.**	many types of seafood and vegetables scattered over rice
11. _____ Wakayama	**k.**	a unique bento served in a *Daruma-shaped* box

Chapter 6

Why is there a 5 o'clock bell?

５時のチャイム

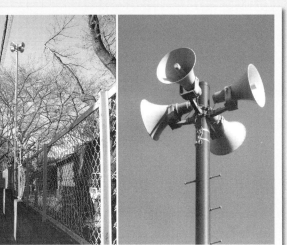

Warm-up Questions

次の質問について考えてみましょう。

1. Have you ever noticed music playing over loudspeakers in your hometown? What time is it played? What song do they play?

2. Why do you think towns all over Japan play music over loudspeakers at certain times of the day? What do you think the purpose is? Discuss with your partner and guess possible reasons.

Vocabulary Check

🔊 Audio 16

次の単語の意味を a 〜 i のなかから選びましょう。

1. ＿＿＿ broadcast (*n.*)
2. ＿＿＿ emergency (*n.*)
3. ＿＿＿ earthquake (*n.*)
4. ＿＿＿ sophisticated (*adj.*)
5. ＿＿＿ warning (*n.*)
6. ＿＿＿ vary (*v.*)
7. ＿＿＿ controversial (*adj.*)
8. ＿＿＿ critic (*n.*)
9. ＿＿＿ bothersome (*adj.*)

a. a natural disaster in which the ground shakes violently

b. be different from case to case

c. complex; advanced; high-level

d. causing trouble; annoying; disturbing

e. something about which people disagree; issues which make some people angry

f. a message or announcement that some natural disaster might happen

g. a person who makes negative comments

h. a radio or TV program; a transmitted announcement

i. a dangerous or serious situation

Pre-reading Quiz

本文を読む前に次の質問について答えましょう。

In which decade did the tradition of the daily 5 o'clock bell begin?

a) 1920s **b)** 1940s **c)** 1960s

Reading

A French businessman living in Tokyo is puzzled by the music that is played from outdoor speakers near his office every day at 5 p.m.

Every day in cities and towns across Japan, at the same time every day, music is played for a few minutes over outdoor loudspeakers. This short musical broadcast is usually called the *goji no chaimu* (5 o'clock bell). Most people think the purpose is to let children know it's time to go home, but it is actually a test of
5 the emergency broadcast system.

Emergency broadcast systems were first introduced after a major earthquake struck Niigata in 1964. Today, more than 90 percent of cities, towns and villages in Japan have such systems. They are linked to a sophisticated national system that can transmit warnings to local governments throughout the country in as
10 little as seven seconds. New digital systems, which have been adopted in some communities, can send warnings directly to people's mobile phones, and automatically post information on the local government's Web page.

The daily test is not always at 5 p.m. Some towns do their test in the morning. Others run their tests twice a day, at noon and 6 p.m., for example. But
15 generally the daily test is timed so it serves some other purpose, such as reminding children to go home before dark. In some communities the evening broadcast is timed at 4:30 p.m. in the winter months, and later when the days are longer. The music also varies quite a bit. Traditional Japanese songs like "Yuyake Koyake" are often used, but Western music is popular too.

20 Some local governments use the emergency broadcast system to make non-emergency announcements, but this practice is controversial. While it can be useful for letting people know about community events, critics say there are better ways to do this. The noise of the announcements can be bothersome, particularly for people who work at night and need to sleep during the day.

✏ 302 words

ⓃⓄ🅣Ⓔ🅢 |||||||||||||||||||||||||||||||||||||||||||||||||||||||||||||||||||||||||||||||||||||||||||||||||
l. 2: loudspeaker 拡声器 l. 9: transmit 伝える local government 地方自治体 l. 12: post 掲示する l. 14: run（実験などを）実施する

Reading Comprehension: True or False

本文で述べられていることについて正しいものに T、間違っているものに F を選び○で囲みましょう。

1. (T F) The main purpose of the 5 o'clock bell is to tell children it's time to go home.

2. (T F) The daily test of the emergency broadcast system is at 5 p.m. in every city.

3. (T F) Some people dislike the use of the emergency broadcast system for other announcements.

Listening: Dialogue

🔊 **Audio 18**

次の会話を聴き、空所を埋めましょう。

Trey asks Akiko about the music he hears playing over the loudspeaker.

Trey: Hey, can I ask you something? What's that music playing over the loudspeaker?

Akiko: Oh, that song? It's ①_____ "Yuyake Koyake." It's a Japanese children's ②_____ song.

Trey: Yes, I know the song, but it ③_____ _____ I hear it around this time every day.

Akiko: Yeah, many Japanese ④_____ and _____ play it every day. Isn't it annoying?

Trey: No, ⑤_____ _____ _____. I think it has a soothing melody and it ⑥_____ me. But what's the purpose of playing it every day?

Akiko: Most people think it's to tell children it's ⑦_____ _____ _____ _____, but actually the main reason is to test the emergency broadcast system.

Trey: Oh, that ⑧_____ _____. So every city in Japan plays the same song at the same time?

Akiko: No, actually it varies. I've even heard of one ⑨_____ village that plays it at 6 in the morning!

Trey: Oh, I'm not a ⑩_____ _____, so that would be annoying!

True or False

もう一度会話を聴き、正しいものに T を、間違っているものに F を○で囲みましょう。

1. (T F) Trey likes the song "Yuyake Koyake."

2. (T F) Every place in Japan plays the same song to test the emergency broadcast system.

3. (T F) Trey likes getting up early in the morning.

Grammar Check

会話に出てきた表現を確認しながら （　　　） 内の適切な語を選びましょう。

1. It (ⓐ seem ⓑ seems) like it's going to rain, so you should bring an umbrella.

2. That song has a (ⓐ relaxing ⓑ relaxes) melody. It really makes me feel (ⓐ relaxing ⓑ relaxed).

3. (ⓐ Almost ⓑ Most) Japanese people know the song "Yuyake Koyake."

パートナーと次のトピックについて話し合ってみましょう。

1. Imagine you were on a committee to choose the song to be played each day to test the emergency broadcast system in your town. What song would you choose? Why?

2. What is your opinion about playing music over the public broadcast system every day? Circle your opinion from the choices and defend your answer. A) The system should continue as it is, with one daily test. B) It's fine to use the system for general announcements to local citizens, too. C) The daily test over loudspeakers is not necessary. Local governments should use other methods of sending information.

Topic Expansion

Japan has been using the emergency broadcast system since the 1960s to help warn people during a natural disaster. Match each word with the correct definition.

1. _____ blackout

2. _____ blizzard

3. _____ drought

4. _____ evacuation area

5. _____ flood

6. _____ hurricane

7. _____ landslide

8. _____ tornado

9. _____ typhoon

10. _____ volcanic eruption

a. a place where people can go to be safe after a natural disaster

b. a storm with heavy rain and wind which comes from the Atlantic Ocean

c. a storm with heavy rain and wind which comes from the Pacific Ocean

d. a situation where the water raises to dangerous levels after heavy rainfall

e. a situation where there is not enough water due to a lack of rainfall

f. when the electricity goes out because of some extreme weather or disaster

g. violent columns of wind which usually come from thunderstorms

h. when steam and other dangerous materials come out of a volcano

i. a heavy snowstorm

j. when earth or rocks fall from a mountain or cliff

指差呼称

Warm-up Questions

次の質問について考えてみましょう。

1. How do you usually get around in your daily life? Do you drive? Do you take public transportation, such as trains, subways, or buses? Or do you get around mostly by bicycle?

2. It is often said that Japan has one of the best train systems in the world. Do you agree? Why or why not? What are the good points of trains in Japan?

Vocabulary Check

🔊 Audio 19

次の単語の意味を a ～ j のなかから選びましょう。

1. _____ reduce (*v.*)
2. _____ error (*n.*)
3. _____ mental (*adj.*)
4. _____ confirm (*v.*)
5. _____ alert (*adj.*)
6. _____ task (*n.*)
7. _____ prevent (*v.*)
8. _____ employee (*n.*)
9. _____ method (*n.*)
10. _____ embarrassed (*adj.*)

a. another word for mistake
b. connected to the brain or thinking; not the body
c. job or piece of work
d. stop something from happening
e. make something happen less frequently
f. a person who works for a company
g. feeling of shyness or not wanting to do something
h. check something again
i. way of doing something
j. feeling awake or focused

Pre-reading Quiz

本文を読む前に次の質問について答えましょう。

For how many years have railway company employees in Japan used "pointing and calling"（指差喚呼）?

a) about 25 years **b)** about 50 years **c)** more than 100 years

An Indian student living in Osaka wonders why conductors on Japanese trains talk to themselves and make strange hand gestures.

That's a method for improving safety by reducing human error. It's called *shisa kanko* (pointing and calling) and improves workers' mental focus at key points where accidents are likely to occur. Here's how it works: Let's say it's your job to make sure a valve is open. You look directly at the valve and confirm that

5 it's open. You call out in a clear voice, "Valve open!" Then, while looking at the valve, you draw your hand back, point to the valve and call out, "OK!" As you do this, you are using your muscles and hearing your own voice. This stimulates your brain to make you more alert.

According to one study, workers asked to complete a simple task made 2.38

10 errors per 100 actions when no special steps were taken to prevent errors. When told to add just calling or just pointing, their error rate dropped significantly. But the greatest reduction in error — to just 0.38 mistakes per 100 actions — was achieved when workers used both steps together. The combination of pointing and calling reduced mistakes by almost 85 percent.

15 Japanese railway employees have been using the pointing-and-calling technique for more than 100 years, and it's been adopted in many other industries in Japan as well. Yet this useful method for reducing human error is hardly known outside of Japan. Some Japanese companies tried to introduce it in their factories in other countries, but it wasn't well accepted by workers. It seems they

20 felt embarrassed to have to point and make the calls. Even in Japan, workers tend to feel embarrassed at first, but it's hard to argue with the results. How might you use this technique in your own daily life? Why not try using it to reduce common mistakes, such as leaving home without your key?

🖊 300 words

NOTES ||||||||||||||||||||||||||||||||||||||||||||||||||||||||||||||||||||||||||||||||||||||||||||||||||||||||
l. 17: as well: (文尾で) =too   l. 21: argue with: (事実・意見) に異議をとなえる、を否定する

Reading Comprehension: True or False

本文で述べられていることについて正しいものに T、間違っているものに F を選び○で囲みましょう。

1. (T F) The purpose of pointing and calling is to reduce the number of accidents.

2. (T F) When workers make both a call and a physical action, errors are reduced at a higher rate.

3. (T F) Pointing and calling has been widely accepted outside of Japan.

Listening: Dialogue

🔊 Audio 21

次の会話を聴き、空所を埋めましょう。

Jason and Junko are riding the train together in Japan.

Junko: What's wrong? What are you ①_____ _____?

Jason: The train conductor! What in the world is she doing? She looks like she's ②_____ _____ _____.

Junko: Oh, actually that's very important. It's a safety method known as ③_____ and _____.

Jason: What's the ④_____ of _____? Does it really work?

Junko: It does! Research shows that both speaking aloud and pointing ⑤_____ workers more ⑥_____.

Jason: Really? I wasn't ⑦_____ of that. So, is it a new technique?

Junko: No. In fact, it has a history of over 100 years. It's used in other industries as well. Do you think it would ⑧_____ _____ in your country?

Jason: No, I doubt it. I think people would just feel embarrassed doing ⑨_____ a _____.

Junko: Well, they should at least try it. It's better to be ⑩_____ than _____!

True or False

もう一度会話を聴き、正しいものに T を、間違っているものに F を○で囲みましょう。

1. (T F) At first, Jason thinks pointing and calling looks strange.

2. (T F) Pointing and calling is a new technique for safety in Japan.

3. (T F) Jason thinks pointing and calling would be popular in his country.

Grammar Check

会話に出てきた表現を確認しながら （　　　）内の適切な語を選びましょう。

1. "Pointing and calling" is a (ⓐ safe ⓑ safety) method used in industries in Japan.

2. I'm always alert when I'm driving, so I think I'm a (ⓐ safe ⓑ safety) driver.

3. When I'm home alone, I sometimes talk to (ⓐ myself ⓑ oneself).

4. I tried using the copy machine, but it (ⓐ don't ⓑ doesn't) work.

Discussion Questions

パートナーと次のトピックについて話し合ってみましょう。

1. How would you feel if you had to do "pointing and calling" for your job? Would you feel embarrassed? Or would you feel proud to use such an effective safety method?

2. Train drivers and conductors help people move safely from their homes to their jobs or schools. Would you like a job with so much responsibility? Why or why not?

Read the clues and fill in the correct answers from the list of words provided.

Trains and Stations

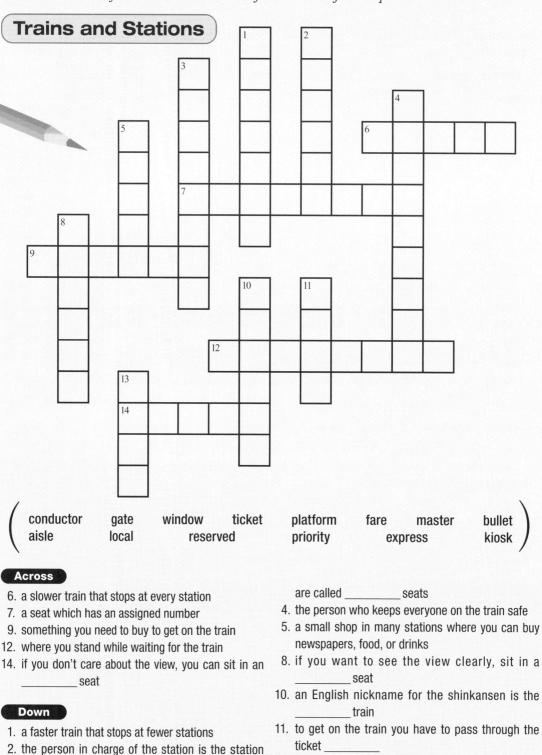

conductor gate window ticket platform fare master bullet
aisle local reserved priority express kiosk

Across

6. a slower train that stops at every station
7. a seat which has an assigned number
9. something you need to buy to get on the train
12. where you stand while waiting for the train
14. if you don't care about the view, you can sit in an _____ seat

Down

1. a faster train that stops at fewer stations
2. the person in charge of the station is the station _____
3. special seats for elderly or pregnant passengers are called _____ seats
4. the person who keeps everyone on the train safe
5. a small shop in many stations where you can buy newspapers, food, or drinks
8. if you want to see the view clearly, sit in a _____ seat
10. an English nickname for the shinkansen is the _____ train
11. to get on the train you have to pass through the ticket _____
13. if you need to pay extra for your ticket, use the _____ adjustment machine

Chapter 8

How is nori made?

海苔

Warm-up Questions

次の質問について考えてみましょう。

1. Which do you prefer, sushi rice with fish on top (*nigiri-zushi*) or sushi rice with fish rolled with nori (*maki-zushi*)? Why?

2. How often do you eat nori? Try to think of at least five foods you eat that are made with nori.

Vocabulary Check

🔊 Audio 22

次の単語の意味を a 〜 i のなかから選びましょう。

1. _____ edible (*adj.*)	**a.** not deep, such as with water
2. _____ shallow (*adj.*)	**b.** cut into small pieces with a knife or other sharp tools
3. _____ fertilizer (*n.*)	**c.** transfer a liquid from one container to another
4. _____ cultivate (*v.*)	**d.** make something last for a long time
5. _____ preserve (*v.*)	**e.** a substance that helps a plant grow
6. _____ chop (*v.*)	**f.** suitable or safe to be eaten
7. _____ pour (*v.*)	**g.** the feel of an object or food
8. _____ texture (*n.*)	**h.** how hot or cold something is
9. _____ temperature (*n.*)	**i.** prepare or try to make something grow

Pre-reading Quiz

本文を読む前に次の質問について答えましょう。

Dried nori was developed using techniques borrowed from what other craft?

a) tea-making **b)** tatami-making **c)** paper-making

A visitor from Holland, enjoying rolled sushi at a party, asks what nori is and how it's made.

Nori is an edible seaweed that grows naturally on rocks in the shallow, coastal areas of cold oceans. People in Japan have gathered it for thousands of years, using it for both food and fertilizer. Then in the early 18th century, fishermen in Edo (present-day Tokyo) discovered a way to cultivate nori. They
5　placed bamboo sticks upright into the bay, creating a place for the plant to attach and grow. To harvest, they would row out in boats and collect the nori off the sticks.

Until then, nori had been eaten fresh, but drawing on techniques used in traditional paper-making, the fishermen also invented a method to dry and
10　preserve their production. This is nori as we know it today: paper-thin dried sheets that keep well and are perfect for wrapping around rice. To make nori using this traditional method, you first chop the plant and mix it with water. This is poured into a wooden frame held over a woven mat. When the water drains away, the frame is removed. What remains on the mat is a thin layer of chopped
15　seaweed that is set out in the sun to dry.

Tokyo was once the top nori producer in Japan, but now the most important production areas are in Kyushu around the Ariake Sea, in Mie and Aichi prefectures around Ise Bay, and around the Inland Sea. The taste, color and texture of dried nori can vary widely, depending, in part, on the temperature of
20　the seawater in which it is grown. The sheets of nori you buy in stores are called *yakinori* and have been toasted. You can also buy *ajitsukenori*, which is flavored with soy sauce, sugar and other seasonings. Nori is a healthy food that contains protein, fiber and vitamins. And it has hardly any calories!

✏ 300 words

Ⓝⓞⓣⓔⓢ ||||||||||||||||||||||||||||||||||||||||||||||||||||||||||||||||||||||||||||||||||||||||||
l. 2: coastal 沿岸の　　gather 収穫する　　l. 10: paper-thin とても薄い　　l. 13: woven: (ひも・糸などを) 編んで作った
l. 13-14 drain away: (食物などの水気) を切る

Reading Comprehension: True or False

本文で述べられていることについて正しいものに T、間違っているものに F を選び○で囲みましょう。

1. (T F) Nori grows in the deep parts of the sea.

2. (T F) Water is used when making dried nori.

3. (T F) Tokyo is still one of the top producers of nori in Japan.

Listening: Dialogue

🔊 **Audio 24**   海苔

次の会話を聴き、空所を埋めましょう。

Makoto notices Jean isn't eating the nori that comes with her onigiri.

Makoto: What are you doing? Why are you ① _____ the nori ② _____ your *onigiri*?

Jean: Oh, is that ③ _____? I thought it was just a ④ _____! I don't usually eat that part.

Makoto: How come? It's just dried seaweed. You ⑤ _____ _____ _____.

Jean: Dried seaweed? Actually, I've ⑥ _____ _____ seaweed in my life. It's not for me.

Makoto: Well, ⑦ _____ _____ _____ know if you've never tried it? You might like it.

Jean: I just don't think I'd like it. I'm a really ⑧ _____ _____.

Makoto: Just take a bite. It has a nice texture and also lots of ⑨ _____ and ⑩ _____.

Jean: OK, I'll try it. Wow, that's ⑪ _____ _____ at all. I should be more open-minded.

Makoto: That's right. You'll never know if you like something ⑫ _____ you try it.

True or False

もう一度会話を聴き、正しいものに T を、間違っているものに F を○で囲みましょう。

1. (T F) Jean already knew that nori is edible.

2. (T F) Jean is interested in new foods and is excited to try nori.

3. (T F) In the end, Jean decides she likes the taste of nori.

Grammar Check

会話に出てきた表現を確認しながら（　　　）内の適切な語を選びましょう。

1. You should take (ⓐ off ⓑ out) your shoes before entering that room.

2. (ⓐ How ⓑ Why) come you don't like seaweed? It tastes good.

3. You should always keep an (ⓐ open mind ⓑ open-minded) about new foods.

4. I like all music (ⓐ except ⓑ unless) pop music.

Discussion Questions

パートナーと次のトピックについて話し合ってみましょう。

1. Are there foods you disliked at first but came to like? What made you change your mind?

2. Have you tried any strange or exotic foods? What were they? Did you like them? Are there any strange or exotic foods that you haven't eaten before but would like to try?

Topic Expansion

Sushi in English

Match the Japanese names with the English names on the right.

1. _____ *ebi*
2. _____ *hamachi*
3. _____ *hotate*
4. _____ *ika*
5. _____ *iwashi*
6. _____ *kani*
7. _____ *maguro*
8. _____ *saba*
9. _____ *tako*
10. _____ *toro*
11. _____ *unagi*
12. _____ uni

a. octopus
b. tuna
c. tuna belly
d. crab
e. yellowtail
f. scallop
g. mackerel
h. sardine
i. sea urchin
j. eel
k. squid
l. shrimp

Chapter 9

What are those exercises Japanese do together?

ラジオ体操

Warm-up Questions

次の質問について考えてみましょう。

1. When you were a child, did you like or dislike doing radio exercises? Why?

2. How often do you exercise now? What kinds of exercise do you usually do?

Vocabulary Check

🔊 **Audio 25**

次の単語の意味を a 〜 j のなかから選びましょう。

1. _____ broadcast (*v.*)	**a.** become popular; spread
2. _____ catch on (*v.*)	**b.** take part in or do something
3. _____ participate (*v.*)	**c.** advantage or good point of something
4. _____ drive (*n.*)	**d.** an area within a town or city where people live near each other
5. _____ neighborhood (*n.*)	**e.** give support or advice; try to get someone to do something
6. _____ encourage (*v.*)	**f.** transmit information or entertainment on the radio or television
7. _____ senior citizen (*n.*)	**g.** an effort by a group of people to achieve something
8. _____ silly (*adj.*)	**h.** the ability to bend the body easily
9. _____ benefit (*n.*)	**i.** foolish; funny
10. _____ flexibility (*n.*)	**j.** a retired or elderly person

---

Pre-reading Quiz

本文を読む前に次の質問について答えましょう。

When was the first radio exercise program broadcast in Japan?

a) 1925 **b)** 1928 **c)** 1946

Reading

A student from the Philippines in Japan is woken every morning by loud music in the park next to her dormitory. She goes to see and is surprised to find people of all ages exercising together. Her Japanese friend explains.

The people in the park were doing *rajio taisō*, which literally means "radio exercises." It is a series of simple calisthenics performed to piano music and spoken instruction. Just about every Japanese knows this exercise routine because it is taught in schools, and is broadcast on radio and television every day. But here's
5 something not many people know: the idea originally came from the United States!

The first radio exercise program in the world was broadcast in 1925 in New York, sponsored by an American life insurance company. The program didn't catch on in the United States, but a Japanese study group picked up the idea and brought it back to Japan. On the morning of November 1, 1928, the first *rajio*
10 *taisō* program was broadcast in Tokyo. By 1932, over 1.5 million Japanese were doing radio calisthenics every morning. China has something similar but there's nothing like it in most countries around the world.

In Japan, the link between radio calisthenics and elementary schools was forged early, when the central radio station began to broadcast the exercise
15 program at schools during summer vacation. Over 3.5 million people participated, and a drive to get children to exercise to the radio broadcasts went national. Many neighborhoods still organize morning exercises to encourage elementary school students to get up early during summer vacation.

It's not just children who do these exercises. Some companies have their
20 employees start the work day by doing the workout together. And many senior citizens do the exercises, either in groups or at home to their own radio or television. Some adults feel silly doing the movements they learned as children. Others, however, point to the benefits of this simple exercise routine. It engages all the major muscle groups, improves posture and flexibility, and even boosts the
25 metabolism to promote weight loss.

304 words

NOTES ||||||||||||||||||||||||||||||||||||||||||||||||||||||||||||||||||||||||||||||||||||||||||||||||||||||||
l. 2: calisthenics 自分の体重を使った筋力トレーニング　l. 3: routine 一連の決められた動作　l. 14: be forged 構築された、結びつけられた　ll. 16-17: go national 全国的なものになる　l. 24: boost 高める、上げる　l. 25: metabolism 代謝

Reading Comprehension: True or False

本文で述べられていることについて正しいものに T、間違っているものに F を選び○で囲みましょう。

1. (T　F)　The first radio exercise program in the world was broadcast in Tokyo.
2. (T　F)　Many countries in the world now have radio exercise programs.
3. (T　F)　Radio calisthenics are now done by people of all ages in Japan.

Listening: Dialogue

🔊 **Audio 27**

次の会話を聴き、空所を埋めましょう。

Grace is job hunting in Japan and asks Akio about his workplace.

Grace: Do you mind if I ask you a question about working for a Japanese company? Do all ① _____ have to do radio exercises together?

Akio: No way! Some companies ② _____ _____ _____, but I wouldn't want to work for such a company!

Grace: Oh, why not? It ③ _____ _____ a great way to start the day!

Akio: I'm ④ _____ _____ _____ about that. I would feel ⑤ _____ exercising at work.

Grace: Not me. It sounds like a fun way to ⑥ _____ and ⑦ _____ with my co-workers.

Akio: It does have some benefits, but I ⑧ _____ to keep work and exercise separate.

Grace: But I ⑨ _____ _____ even famous people like Hayao Miyazaki are into radio exercises. Studio Ghibli ⑩ _____ do radio exercises together every day!

Akio: Well, if I had the chance to work at Studio Ghibli, I guess I could ⑪ _____ _____ _____ doing radio exercises!

True or False

もう一度会話を聴き、正しいものに T を、間違っているものに F を○で囲みましょう。

1. (T F) Akio's company requires workers to do radio exercises together.

2. (T F) Grace thinks that doing radio exercises at work is a good idea.

3. (T F) Akio likes to exercise while he is at work.

Grammar Check

会話に出てきた表現を確認しながら（　　　）内の適切な語を選びましょう。

1. Do you mind if I (ⓐ open ⓑ opening) the window? It's hot in here.

2. I (ⓐ won't ⓑ wouldn't) want to work for a company that requires too much overtime.

3. I always (ⓐ feel ⓑ feeling) great after a morning workout.

4. I (ⓐ am prefer ⓑ prefer) living in the country to living in a big city.

Discussion Questions

パートナーと次のトピックについて話し合ってみましょう。

1. Imagine you are working for a company and there is a proposal to do radio exercises together every morning. Would you be for or against this proposal? Explain your reasons.

2. These days, many children don't eat well or get enough exercise. For example, the number of elementary school children who participate in radio exercises has greatly decreased. How do you think we can encourage children to eat a healthy diet and exercise more?

Read the clues and fill in the correct answers from the list of words provided.

Health and Fitness

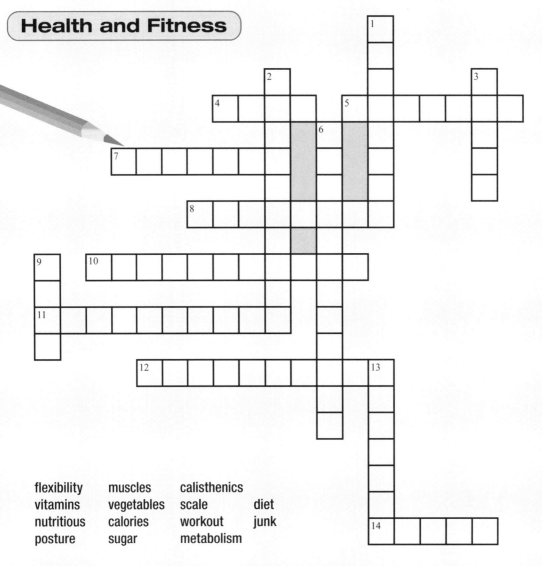

flexibility	muscles	calisthenics	
vitamins	vegetables	scale	diet
nutritious	calories	workout	junk
posture	sugar	metabolism	

Across

4. what you go on if you want to lose weight
5. another word for exercise or training
7. the position in which you hold your body while sitting or standing
8. pills people take to help them stay healthy
10. the ability to easily bend your body
11. another word for healthy food or meals
12. the process by which your body changes food into energy
14. the instrument you step on to check your weight

Down

1. if you want to lose weight, you should count these carefully
2. plants or parts of plants that healthy people may eat a lot of
3. something that makes food sweet but you should not eat too much of
6. gymnastic exercises that are good for making a fit body
9. if you are worried about your health, you should avoid eating too much _____ food
13. tissues in your body that keep it strong

賞味期限

Warm-up Questions

次の質問について考えてみましょう。

1. When you go shopping, do you check the times and dates listed on the food packages? Why or why not?

2. Have you ever eaten something after the expiry date? If so, how long after was it? Did you get sick?

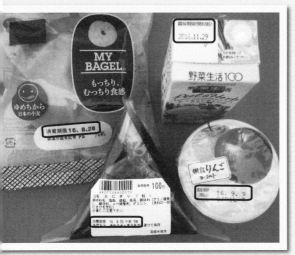

Vocabulary Check

🔊 Audio 28

次の語（句）の意味を a ～ j のなかから選びましょう。

1. _____ expiry (*n.*)
2. _____ throw out (*v.*)
3. _____ perishable (*adj.*)
4. _____ shelf life (*n.*)
5. _____ unpleasant (*adj.*)
6. _____ obvious (*adj.*)
7. _____ spoilage (*n.*)
8. _____ waste (*n.*)
9. _____ household (*n.*)
10. _____ starving (*adj.*)

a. garbage; trash
b. the end of the period for which something is good
c. without enough food to survive or be a healthy
d. not agreeable; feels, looks, or smells bad
e. the amount of something that has gone bad and shouldn't be eaten anymore
f. group of family members who live together
g. plain; easy to see
h. the period of time for which a food product is safe to eat
i. possible to go bad, especially food
j. put something into the trash or garbage

Pre-reading Quiz

本文を読む前に次の質問について答えましょう。

How much food waste do you think is produced in Japan each year?

a) hundreds of tons **b)** thousands of tons **c)** millions of tons

Reading

A student from England wants to know if the rice ball he bought yesterday is safe to eat. What does the date on the package mean?

There are two types of expiry dates used on food packages in Japan: *shōhi kigen* and *shōmi kigen*. They mean different things and are used on different foods. Unfortunately, most consumers don't understand the difference. As a result, they throw out food that is still perfectly safe to eat. *Shōhi kigen* means
5 "limit for consumption" and corresponds to "use by" labeling in English. This type of expiry date is used on highly perishable products, including bento meals, sandwiches and cakes made with fresh whipped cream. These expiry dates should be taken seriously because such foods go bad quickly after their "use by" date.

The other type of expiry date is *shōmi kigen*, which means "limit for best
10 taste." This is similar to "best by" labeling in English. *Shōmi kigen* is used on products that have a long shelf life, including potato chips, instant noodles and canned food. You're unlikely to get sick if you eat these foods after the date on the package, although they might not taste as good as when fresh. Keep in mind, however, that there are also moderately perishable foods, including milk, eggs,
15 ham and tofu, that are labeled with *shōmi kigen* ("best by") rather than *shōhi kigen* ("use by"). These foods are safe to eat for some days after the *shōmi kigen* date on the package.

It's easy to tell when such foods have gone bad because they produce unpleasant smells or other obvious signs of spoilage. Every year, Japan produces
20 millions of tons of food waste. About half comes from households who buy more than they need and throw out food when it's still safe to eat. That's not only a waste of money, it's also bad for the environment and a real shame with so many starving people in the world.

🖊 298 words

N⃝O⃝T⃝E⃝S⃝ ||||||||||||||||||||||||||||||||||||||||||||||||||||||||||||||||||||||||||||||||||||||||||||||||||||||||||||||||||||||
l. 5: correspond to ～に該当する   l. 14: moderately 非常に   perishable: 腐りやすい   l. 21: throw out: 捨てる

Reading Comprehension: True or False

本文で述べられていることについて正しいものに T、間違っているものに F を選び○で囲みましょう。

1. (T F) *Shōhi kigen* and *shōmi kigen* have basically the same meaning.
2. (T F) You will probably get sick if you eat a food after the *shōmi kigen* date.
3. (T F) Many Japanese people buy more food than they actually need.

Listening: Dialogue 🔊 Audio 30

賞味期限

次の会話を聴き、空所を埋めましょう。

Kevin and Mika are talking about whether or not to throw away food.

Kevin: Hey, what are you doing? You're not ① _____ _____ that yogurt, are you?

Mika: Yeah, the ② _____ _____ was yesterday, so it might be spoiled. I don't want to get sick.

Kevin: Oh, come on! That's just the ③ _____ _____ _____. There's no way you'll get sick from it. Don't throw it out.

Mika: Why do you care so much? You ④ _____ _____ like yogurt!

Kevin: That's not the point. There are ⑤ _____ of starving people in the world.

Mika: So what? It's just one container of yogurt. It's not a ⑥ _____ _____.

Kevin: I just don't like to see people ⑦ _____ food. Besides, all that ⑧ _____ is also bad for the environment.

Mika: Give me a break. I'm sure people in your country waste a lot ⑨ _____ _____.

Kevin: That ⑩ _____ _____ _____, but wasted food is wasted food. It's never a good thing.

Mika: OK, I'll just eat it then. But I ⑪ _____ _____ get sick!

True or False

もう一度会話を聴き、正しいものにTを、間違っているものにFを○で囲みましょう。

1. (T F) Mika thinks that the yogurt is still safe to eat.
2. (T F) Kevin thinks that Mika should throw the yogurt out.
3. (T F) In the end, Mika decides to eat the yogurt.

Grammar Check

会話に出てきた表現を確認しながら（　　）内の適切な語を選びましょう。

1. This smells terrible. You should (ⓐ throw ⓑ throwing) it out!
2. I'm sure we'll win the game. There's (ⓐ no ⓑ not a) way we'll lose.
3. I wish I could win (ⓐ a million ⓑ millions) of dollars in the lottery.
4. It's never (ⓐ a good thing ⓑ good things) to lose your temper.

パートナーと次のトピックについて話し合ってみましょう。

1. Do you sometimes waste food? Do you often see other people wasting food? Why do you think this happens? Can you think of any ways to reduce the amount of wasted food? Share your ideas with your partners.

2. In recent years, there have been some expiry date scandals. For example, some companies put a fake expiry date on their products so they could sell them for a longer period of time than allowed. Do you trust the expiry dates on food? Why or why not?

Topic Expansion

Matching Perishable and Non-Perishable Foods

As you read in this unit, many people throw away food even when it's still safe to eat. Put the foods in the list into the proper category in the chart.

Perishable Foods (foods that spoil quickly and require refrigeration)	**Non-Perishable Foods** (foods with a long shelf life that don't usually require refrigeration)

Food List

canned fruits and vegetables	canned seafood	cheese
cooked leftovers	eggs	fresh fruits and vegetables
fruit juice	ketchup	meat
milk	oatmeal	pasta
peanut butter	rice	fresh seafood
soy sauce		

Chapter 11

Why do Japanese ask about blood type?

Warm-up Questions

次の質問について考えてみましょう。

1. When you meet someone for the first time, what kind of questions do you usually ask them? What information do you want to know first?

2. How would you describe your own personality? For example, do you think you're a serious person? Shy? Lively? Outgoing? Describe your personality to your partners.

Vocabulary Check

Audio 31

次の単語の意味を a 〜 j のなかから選びましょう。

1. _____ personality (*n.*)
2. _____ determine (*v.*)
3. _____ element (*n.*)
4. _____ inherit (*v.*)
5. _____ sensitive (*adj.*)
6. _____ originate (*v.*)
7. _____ attempt (*n.*)
8. _____ superiority (*n.*)
9. _____ race (*n.*)
10. _____ random (*adj.*)

a. begin; start
b. easily annoyed or hurt; aware of others' feelings
c. get something from your parents
d. without reason; by chance
e. a group of people identified as different from other groups because of shared physical or genetic traits
f. effort; try
g. a component or part of
h. decide; conclude
i. quality of being better than all others
j. the character of a person

Pre-reading Quiz

本文を読む前に次の質問について答えましょう。

What is the most common blood type in Japan?

a) A **b)** B **c)** AB **d)** O

An American studying in Japan wants to know why Japanese are so interested in her blood type. She has no idea what her blood type is, because she's always been healthy, and thinks it's a very strange thing to ask.

In Japan, nearly everybody knows their own blood type. The reason for this is a popular belief that personality is determined by blood type. As you may remember from science class, all blood is made up of the same elements, but not all blood is alike. There are four types — A, O, B and AB — which vary
5 depending on the absence or presence of certain inherited substances. Although there is no scientific basis for linking personality and blood type, many Japanese people believe you can learn something about someone by knowing their blood type. According to this thinking, a person with Type A blood, for example, will be *kinben* (diligent), *kireizuki* (neat) and sensitive to the feelings of others.

10 Where did such ideas originate? In Europe, actually. In the 1910s and 20s, some researchers looked at blood type in an attempt to prove the superiority of some races over others. Later, the theme was picked up in Japan. But it wasn't until the 1970s, when a writer named Masahiko Nomi wrote a series of popular books, that the idea of linking blood type to personality became popular.

15 There are two reasons such theories caught on in Japan. One is a traditional belief that hereditary traits are passed on through the blood. The other is that, unlike in some countries, there is a relatively balanced distribution of blood types within the Japanese population: approximately 40 percent Type A; 30 percent Type O; 20 percent Type B and 10 percent Type AB. This means even a random
20 guess will have a fair chance of being correct. Of course, blood type should never be used as the basis for important decisions, such as choosing a marriage partner. But when a Japanese person asks about blood type, it's usually just an attempt to be friendly.

✏ 301 words

Ⓝⓞⓣⓔⓢ
l. 15: catch on (考えなどが) 受ける、流行する   l. 16: trait 特性、特徴   l. 20: chance = possibility

Reading Comprehension: True or False

本文で述べられていることについて正しいものに T、間違っているものに F を選び○で囲みましょう。

1. (T F)   There is scientific proof that blood type and personality are linked.
2. (T F)   The theory linking blood type and personality originated in Europe.
3. (T F)   The writer believes that blood type is a good factor for making important decisions.

Listening: Dialogue

🔊 **Audio 33**

次の会話を聴き、空所を埋めましょう。

Ashley and Ken are discussing blood types.

Ken: Can I ask your blood type? I'll bet you're type O, ① _____ _____?

Ashley: That's right, but why do you think that? What makes you ② _____ _____?

Ken: Because you're a self-starter and tend to do things your ③ _____ _____.

Ashley: Well, that may be true, but it ④ _____ _____ to do with my blood type.

Ken: So you don't ⑤ _____ that your blood type determines your personality?

Ashley: Not at all. That's just ⑥ _____ like horoscopes and ⑦ _____ _____.

Ken: But I ⑧ _____ _____ that you are type O! So why don't you believe in it?

Ashley: Because your personality ⑨ _____ _____. For example, my uncle used to be really selfish. But after he got sick, he became a much nicer person.

Ken: Well, I never thought of that. We ⑩ _____ change our blood type, but we ⑪ _____ change our personality.

True or False

もう一度会話を聴き、正しいものに T を、間違っているものに F を○で囲みましょう。

1. (T F) Ken guesses Ashley's blood type correctly.

2. (T F) Ashley and Ken both believe there's a connection between blood type and personality.

3. (T F) Ashley believes that people can change their personality.

Grammar Check

会話に出てきた表現を確認しながら（　　　）内の適切な語を選びましょう。

1. You have an older sister, (ⓐ aren't ⓑ don't) you?

2. I'm very independent. I like to do things (ⓐ my own way ⓑ my pace).

3. Do you (ⓐ believe ⓑ believing) in fortune telling?

4. My new teacher is (ⓐ much ⓑ very) friendlier than my last teacher.

パートナーと次のトピックについて話し合ってみましょう。

1. Describe your personality to your partners again. After each person describes their personality, try to guess their blood type. Can you guess correctly?

2. Which factor do you think most determines someone's personality? Rank the following factors from most important (1) to least important (5). When you're finished, compare and discuss your answers with your partners. ➤ parents (   ) **/** life experiences (   ) **/** blood type (   ) **/** star sign (   ) **/** birth order; e.g. oldest or youngest child (   )

Topic Expansion

Blood Type and Personality Chart

Some Japanese believe that your personality is determined by your blood type. Put each personality trait in the chart according to the blood type.

A	B
AB	**O**

ambitious	outgoing	compassionate	passionate	independent
patient	intuitive	popular	loyal	rational
optimistic	stubborn			

Chapter 12

Do Japanese mosquito coils work?

蚊取り線香

Warm-up Questions

次の質問について考えてみましょう。

1. What do you usually do to prevent getting bitten or stung by mosquitoes and other insects?

2. Mosquito coils make many people think of summer. What makes you think of summer in Japan? Tell your partners as many summer things that you can think of.

Vocabulary Check

🔊 **Audio 34**

次の単語の意味を a ～ i のなかから選びましょう。

1. _____ exporter (*n.*)
2. _____ seed (*n.*)
3. _____ import (*v.*)
4. _____ deadly (*adj.*)
5. _____ dose (*n.*)
6. _____ repel (*v.*)
7. _____ irritating (*adj.*)
8. _____ alternative (*n.*)
9. _____ device (*n.*)

a. bring in goods from other countries
b. a person who ships goods to other countries
c. has the possibility to kill
d. a quantity of medicine
e. make go away; drive away
f. annoying; unpleasant
g. a thing or method invented for a specific purpose
h. a different choice or option
i. small part of a plant, flower, or fruit

Pre-reading Quiz

本文を読む前に次の質問について答えましょう。

Which famous Japanese figure had a role in the invention of the mosquito coil?

a) Noguchi Hideyo **b)** Ibuka Masaru **c)** Fukuzawa Yukichi

🗣️ *A tourist from Denmark, visiting Japan in the summer, noticed mosquito coils burning in many homes and restaurants. He wants to know if they really keep mosquitos away. What is in them that mosquitoes don't like?*

Mosquito coils were invented in Japan at the end of the 19th century by a man named Ueyama Eiichiro, who was an exporter of mandarin oranges. Fukuzawa Yukichi, the famous author and statesman and founder of Keio University, introduced him to a seed trader in the United States. This trader
5 offered Ueyama seeds of a flowering plant that he claimed could kill insects.

Ueyama decided to import the seeds and grow the plant in Japan. It was a member of the aster family, and certainly didn't look like a killer. The flowers were white with a yellow center, much like the common daisy. But sure enough, there was something in the flowers that proved deadly to insects. Ueyama called
10 the plant *jyochūgiku*, which means "insect-killing chrysanthemum." At first, he used a powder made from the dried flowers to make incense sticks that would drive away insects when burned. They worked quite well but burned down too quickly, lasting barely 40 minutes. So at his wife's suggestion, Ueyama began to make longer sticks and coil them into a spiral.

15 This was a big success and is still sold today. A single coil provides protection for about seven hours. The active ingredient in mosquito coils is pyrethrin, a powerful insecticide that occurs naturally in the *jyochūgiku* flower and can now be synthesized. In small doses, it repels insects. In higher concentrations, it kills them by attacking their nervous systems. Although Japanese used to live in
20 homes that were open to the outdoors, there has been a shift to smaller, more tightly constructed homes. In such environments, the smoke from mosquito coils can be irritating. So now there are no-smoke alternatives, including a device that plugs into electric outlets and a spray that can protect a room from mosquitoes for up to 12 hours.

✏️ 301 words

NⓄTⒺS ⫶⫶

l. 7: aster キク科シオン属　l. 8: daisy ヒナギク　l. 10: chrysanthemum キク（の花）　l. 11: incense お香　l. 14: spiral うず巻き状のもの　l. 16: active ingredient《医学》活性要素　pyrethrin 天然の殺虫剤の一つ　l. 18: synthesize 合成する　l. 19: nervous system 神経系　l. 23: plug into ～に差し込む　outlet コンセント　l. 24: up to（最高）～まで

Reading Comprehension: True or False

本文で述べられていることについて正しいものに T、間違っているものに F を選び○で囲みましょう。

1. (T　F) Mosquito coils were invented by Fukuzawa Yukichi.
2. (T　F) Ueyama Eiichiro's wife gave an important suggestion that led to the invention of the mosquito coil.
3. (T　F) There are now alternatives to mosquito coils because of the change in Japanese homes.

蚊取り線香

Listening: Dialogue

🔊 **Audio 36**

次の会話を聴き、空所を埋めましょう。

Noah is visiting Naomi's home and asks about the smoke coming from the mosquito coil.

Noah: What's that smoke coming from over there? It ① _____ _____ of bad.

Naomi: Oh, sorry, it's just a mosquito coil. Does the ② _____ _____ you?

Noah: Just a little. I have a really sensitive nose, so it's a bit irritating. By the way, do they really ③ _____ the mosquitoes ④ _____ ?

Naomi: Yeah, they're great. I've been using ⑤ _____ _____ _____ .

Noah: But are they safe for ⑥ _____ ? Don't they contain harmful ⑦ _____ ?

Naomi: No, they're perfectly safe ⑧ _____ _____ _____ you use them in a well-ventilated place. I always keep the window open.

Noah: Come to think of it, they do seem to work well. Actually, I haven't ⑨ _____ _____ by a mosquito all night!

Naomi: ⑩ _____ _____ _____ mosquito coils in your country? I thought they were used all over the world.

Noah: Maybe they are, but I've always used ⑪ _____ _____ . But the smell of that bothers me too!

True or False

もう一度会話を聴き、正しいものに T を、間違っているものに F を○で囲みましょう。

1. (T F) Noah likes the smell from mosquito coils.

2. (T F) Naomi believes that mosquito coils are safe for humans.

3. (T F) Naomi thinks that mosquito coils are only used in Japan.

Grammar Check

会話に出てきた表現を確認しながら（　　　）内の適切な語を選びましょう。

1. What's that strange (ⓐ smell ⓑ smelling) ?

2. Something (ⓐ smelling ⓑ smells) bad in here. I wonder what it is.

3. Does it (ⓐ bother ⓑ bothering) you if I smoke?

4. (ⓐ I'm ⓑ I've) always been a Hanshin Tigers fan.

Discussion Questions

パートナーと次のトピックについて話し合ってみましょう。

1. Do you think mosquito coils are effective? Does your family usually use them? Do they keep mosquitoes away?

2. The reading passage notes that there has been a change in Japanese homes. Is the home you live in now very different from the home your parents grew up in? Your grandparents? How is it different? Which style do you like best?

Topic Expansion

Read the clues and fill in the correct answers from the list of words provided.

Summer

firefly   sunflower   mosquito   festival   garden   fireworks   watermelon
eel   baseball   beach   conditioner   pool   sunburn   swimsuit

Across

2. you go here to swim if you can't go to the sea or ocean; some are even indoors
6. you go here to swim in the sea or ocean
8. a fun event held many places in Japan in summer
9. you might get this if you stay in the sun too long
10. beautiful explosions we watch in the sky during summer
13. a big green and red summer fruit
14. many people eat this fish on a special day in July or August to get strength

Down

1. a small insect that likes to bite people
3. the sport high school students play at Koshien Stadium in August
4. if you're 20 years old, you can enjoy cold drinks at a beer _____
5. a beautiful yellow flower which blooms in July and August
7. if it's too hot at home, you can turn on the air _____
11. what you wear when you go swimming
12. a flying insect that lights up the summer sky

Chapter 13

Why does miso soup move by itself?

おみそ汁のモヤモヤ

Warm-up Questions

次の質問について考えてみましょう。

1. Do you eat miso soup every day? Why or why not?

2. Miso soup varies from family to family and in different parts of Japan. What is your favorite kind of miso soup? What ingredients are in it?

Vocabulary Check

🔊 **Audio 37**

次の単語の意味を a 〜 i のなかから選びましょう。

1. _____ surface (*n.*)
2. _____ exposed (*adj.*)
3. _____ liquid (*n.*)
4. _____ solid (*n.*)
5. _____ grind (*v.*)
6. _____ soybean (*n.*)
7. _____ dissolve (*v.*)
8. _____ broth (*n.*)
9. _____ distinctive (*adj.*)

a. not a solid or a gas, such as water
b. not a liquid or gas; something with the inside filled up
c. unique or different; having special qualities
d. water that has been boiled with meat, fish, or vegetables to make a thin soup
e. crush into smaller pieces
f. a plant-food used in making Japanese foods such as *nattō* and miso
g. separate into different parts; melt
h. upper or outer part
i. without protection

Pre-reading Quiz

本文を読む前に次の質問について答えましょう。

Why can we see cloudy "*moya moya*" in miso soup but not in tea?

a) Tea is too hot. **b)** Miso soup has solid material. **c)** Miso soup is a kind of magic.

A visitor from China wants to know why her miso soup moves around in the bowl. Why does the cloudy part gather in the middle, leaving clear liquid on the sides?

That's a very interesting question! Do you remember learning in science class about convection, which occurs when molecules move from one place to another, taking the heat with them? You probably learned that wind and sea waves, for example, are caused by convection. Well, the movement we see in miso soup,
5 which Japanese people commonly refer to as *moya moya*, is actually an everyday example of convection.

Imagine a cup of tea. The tea in the middle of the cup is hotter than the top because the surface is exposed to cool air. To equalize the temperature, the tea organizes itself into zones called convection cells that rise to the surface and give
10 off heat. The heat loss makes the cells denser than those below them, so they fall back down into the liquid where they get warm again. This is called thermal convection. With a clear liquid like tea, you can't see the convection cells. But miso soup contains small pieces of solid material that move with the cells, making it possible for us to see the movement. Miso is made by grinding cooked soybeans
15 and mixing them with salt, grains and a starter called *kōjikin*. This is allowed to ferment, resulting in a thick paste that can be mixed into clear broth to make a soup called miso *shiru*.

All miso pastes contain insoluble material, such as parts of the soybeans that aren't broken down during processing and fermentation. These solids can't
20 dissolve in the broth and make the soup look cloudy. It is also these solids that give miso soup its distinctive taste, because they contain a wealth of flavor and aroma compounds. If you let the soup sit too long, allowing it to separate, it won't taste as good. So stir lightly before enjoying it!

🖉 299 words

NOTES ||||||||||||||||||||||||||||||||||||||||||||||||||||||||||||||||||||||||||||||||||||||||||||||||||||||||||||||||||||||||||||||||||||||||
l. 2: convection《物理》(熱の) 対流、伝達　molecule《物理・化学》分子　l. 8: equalize 均一にする　l. 9-10: give off (熱などを) 発する　l. 11: thermal 熱の　l. 15: starter スターター (発酵用に培養するバクテリア)　l. 16: ferment 発酵する (させる)　l. 18: insoluble 不溶性の　l. 19: break down 分離する

Reading Comprehension: True or False

本文で述べられていることについて正しいものに T、間違っているものに F を選び○で囲みましょう。

1. (T　F)　The cloudy part in miso soup is caused by the same force that causes wind and sea waves.

2. (T　F)　We can see the cloudy part in miso soup because it also contains solids.

3. (T　F)　If you let miso soup sit a long time, it will taste even better.

Listening: Dialogue

🔊 **Audio 39**

次の会話を聴き、空所を埋めましょう。

Eri and Karl are talking about what they eat for breakfast.

Karl: Is that all you're ①_____ for breakfast? It doesn't look very Japanese!

Eri: What do you mean? I usually just have a ②_____ of _____ or something for breakfast.

Karl: Huh. I thought Japanese people ate rice, fish, and miso soup ③_____

_____.

Eri: Oh, that's just the traditional Japanese breakfast. I ④_____ _____

_____ for that.

Karl: Really? But the traditional breakfast seems ⑤_____ _____ _____

nutritious.

Eri: That may be true, but I usually ⑥_____ _____ something from the

convenience store on the ⑦_____ _____ _____.

Karl: But don't you want to live a ⑧_____ and _____ life?

Eri: Actually, I do have a healthy diet most of the time. But I'm always ⑨_____

_____ _____ in the morning, so I don't have time for a full breakfast.

True or False

もう一度会話を聴き、正しいものに T を、間違っているものに F を○で囲みましょう。

1. (T F) Karl is surprised by what Eri is eating for breakfast.

2. (T F) Eri likes to have a traditional Japanese breakfast every morning.

3. (T F) Overall, Eri says she has a healthy diet.

Grammar Check

会話に出てきた表現を確認しながら（　　　）内の適切な語を選びましょう。

1. What do you usually (ⓐ have ⓑ having) for breakfast?

2. Are you (ⓐ have ⓑ having) eggs for breakfast again?

3. To live a long life, good (ⓐ nutrition ⓑ nutritious) is very important.

4. My grandmother is in her 90s, but she's still in good (ⓐ health ⓑ healthy).

Discussion Questions

パートナーと次のトピックについて話し合ってみましょう。

1. Many families have their own special recipe for miso soup. What's a food made by your parents or grandparents that you would like to pass on to your children?

2. Traditional foods can be very nutritious, but they also take a long time to prepare. When you work full-time in the future, do you want to spend a lot of time preparing meals? Or do you think it's fine to eat fast and simple meals?

おみそ汁のモヤモヤ

Just like Japan has miso soup, many countries in the world have traditional soups. Read the descriptions of traditional soups below and write the correct country from the map in each blank.

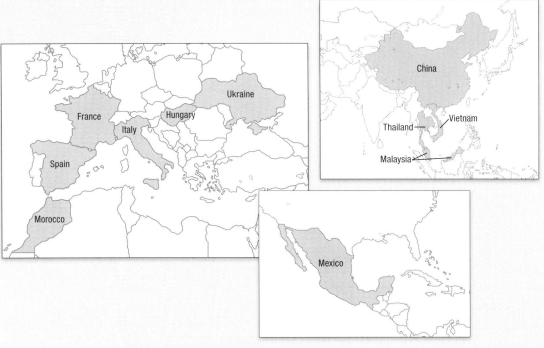

1. _____ **minestrone:** a vegetarian soup with onions, carrots, beans, and tomatoes; sometimes pasta or rice is added

2. _____ **tom yum:** a hot and sour soup containing lemon grass, fish sauce, chilies, and shrimp

3. _____ **bouillabaisse:** a fish stock with fish and shellfish and flavored with ingredients like garlic and basil

4. _____ **borscht:** a dark red-colored soup made from beetroots; popular in countries with long, cold winter

5. _____ **pho:** a beef noodle soup flavored with ginger, coriander, and basil

6. _____ **gazpacho:** a chilled summer soup made with tomatoes, bell pepper, garlic, and olive oil

7. _____ **laksa:** a spicy noodle soup containing chicken, shrimp, or fish; often has a curry coconut milk base

8. _____ **shark fin:** a soup containing shark fin served during special occasions such as weddings

9. _____ **harira:** a popular food among Muslims during Ramadan; contains tomatoes, chickpeas, and meat

10. _____ **goulash:** a spicy soup containing beef, onions, red pepper, and paprika powder

11. _____ **menudo:** a soup containing beef stomach (tripe) with a red chili pepper base

Chapter 14

What are those giant concrete things by the sea?

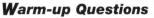

Warm-up Questions

次の質問について考えてみましょう。

1. Do you know what tetrapods are? What do you think their purpose is? Try to explain in English.

2. Have you ever noticed tetrapods along Japan's coast? If so, what's your impression of them? Do you have a positive or negative impression? Why?

Vocabulary Check

🔊 Audio 40

次の単語の意味を a 〜 j のなかから選びましょう。

1. _____ structure (*n.*)	**a.**	put something together
2. _____ crash (*v.*)	**b.**	something built or constructed
3. _____ scatter (*v.*)	**c.**	bad weather condition
4. _____ extreme (*adj.*)	**d.**	move to another place
5. _____ erosion (*n.*)	**e.**	separate into different directions
6. _____ storm (*n.*)	**f.**	change or modify
7. _____ transport (*v.*)	**g.**	process of the earth being worn away
8. _____ mold (*n.*)	**h.**	beyond average or ordinary; not normal
9. _____ assemble (*v.*)	**i.**	collide with another object and make a loud noise
10. _____ alter (*v.*)	**j.**	a frame for making a certain shape

Pre-reading Quiz

本文を読む前に次の質問について答えましょう。

In which country were tetrapods invented?

a) Japan **b)** Chile **c)** France

Reading

A visitor from the Netherlands wants to know about the huge cement structures one sees on Japan's coast. Why are they there? How are they made and transported?

Those cement structures are called "tetrapods," from the Greek meaning "four-legged." That's actually a registered trade name but most people use the term generically. In Japanese, the proper name is *shōha burokku*, which means "wave-breaking block." Tetrapods are used to protect man-made constructions

5 near water, including seawalls, breakwaters and land-reclamation projects like Kansai International Airport, which was built completely out in the water. When placed around a marine construction, tetrapods break incoming waves and redirect the water so it doesn't crash with full force against the construction.

Although tetrapods are a common sight up and down Japan's coastline, they

10 were actually invented in France, in 1949. Until then, coastal engineers used piles of stones or rubble to protect marine constructions. However, that method didn't work well because loose pieces are easily scattered or washed away. Tetrapods work much better because, when arranged in lines or heaps, the legs lock together to create a strong, stable barrier that holds up even under extreme conditions.

15 During Japan's period of high economic growth, tetrapods were widely adopted to slow coastal erosion and protect harbors and fishing ports from storms. Tetrapods became big business, providing work for many engineering and construction companies. Of course, huge cement structures are too heavy to transport — even a small tetrapod weighs close to half a ton. Instead, suppliers

20 lease steel molds to local contractors, who pour the concrete where the tetrapods will be used. Even the molds are huge, too big to transported on Japan's narrow roads. They are delivered in pieces and assembled before the pouring work begins. When the cement is dry, the molds are removed and the tetrapods are lifted into place with cranes. Although many people now regret that so much of Japan's once

25 beautiful coastline has been altered, others find tetrapods oddly beautiful. 🖊300 words

ⓃⓄⓉⒺⓈ ‖‖‖

l. 2: registered trade name 登録商標　l. 5: seawall 堤防　breakwater 防波堤　land-reclamation 埋め立て
l. 6: build out（建物）を建て増しする　l. 7: marine 海上の　incoming wave 寄せ波　l. 8: redirect 〜の向きを変える
l. 9: up and down あちこちに　l. 13: lock together 組み合わさって固定する　l. 20: contractor 土建業者　l. 23-24: into place 所定の位置に

Reading Comprehension: True or False

本文で述べられていることについて正しいものに T、間違っているものに F を選び○で囲みましょう。

1. (T　F)　Tetrapods are mainly used to protect natural scenery.

2. (T　F)　Using piles of stones is an effective way of protecting marine constructions.

3. (T　F)　Tetrapods are very difficult to transport.

Listening: Dialogue

🔊 **Audio 42**

次の会話を聴き、空所を埋めましょう。

Taro and Julia are taking a drive along the coast of Japan and discussing the scenery.

Taro: Isn't the scenery beautiful? What a gorgeous ① _____.

Julia: Yeah, it sure is, ② _____ _____ _____. What are those ugly concrete things all along the sea?

Taro: Oh, you must mean the tetrapods. They're ③ _____ _____ _____ and mysterious, aren't they?

Julia: I'm afraid I disagree. In my opinion, they really ④ _____ the natural ⑤ _____. Do they have a purpose?

Taro: Yes, of course. They protect the harbor and ⑥ _____ _____ erosion. Don't you have them in your country?

Julia: I think we have them, but not so many ⑦ _____ to Japan. In Japan, they're everywhere!

Taro: Actually, I've heard that in some places in Japan they are starting to ⑧ _____ _____.

Julia: That's a ⑨ _____. I understand the purpose of tetrapods, but I just wish there was a ⑩ _____ _____ to protect the coast.

True or False

もう一度会話を聴き、正しいものに T を、間違っているものに F を○で囲みましょう。

1. (T F) Julia thinks everything about the scenery is beautiful.
2. (T F) Taro likes the appearance of tetrapods.
3. (T F) Julia's country has just as many tetrapods as Japan.

Grammar Check

会話に出てきた表現を確認しながら（　　　）内の適切な語を選びましょう。

1. (ⓐ Aren't ⓑ Isn't) this dinner delicious? I made it all by myself.
2. Dogs are wonderful pets, (ⓐ aren't ⓑ isn't) they?
3. It's very important for humans to (ⓐ protect ⓑ protecting) the environment.
4. What a (ⓐ relief ⓑ relieved) that it's not going to rain this weekend.

Discussion Questions

パートナーと次のトピックについて話し合ってみましょう。

1. Imagine you lived along a coastline full of tetrapods. Would you like to keep them there or have them removed? Defend your opinion.
2. Using cement to build structures is huge business in Japan, but some people claim these structures, such as tetrapods, spoil the natural scenery. Which do you think is more important, creating construction jobs or protecting the natural scenery?

Topic Expansion

Read the clues and fill in the correct answers from the list of words provided.

Marine

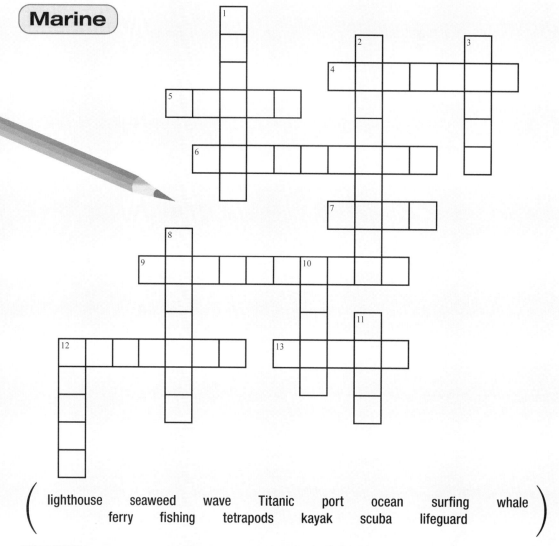

lighthouse   seaweed   wave   Titanic   port   ocean   surfing   whale
ferry   fishing   tetrapods   kayak   scuba   lifeguard

Across

4. nori is an edible type of this
5. a huge mammal which lives in the water
6. a person who saves others if they have some trouble while swimming
7. cities located on the water, such as Kobe and Yokohama, are called _____ towns
9. this tower or structure helps warn or guide ships
12. a sport in which you balance on a board while riding on the water
13. a small narrow boat that you propel with paddles

Down

1. there was a very famous movie about this ship that sank in 1912
2. wave-breaking concrete structures you just read about
3. a boat or ship used to carry passengers across water
8. an activity in which you hope to get some food from the water
10. this water covers about 70 percent of the earth's surface
11. water that breaks into the shore
12. if you want to swim underwater for a long time, try _____ diving

Chapter 15

Why don't more Japanese donate organs?

臓器提供

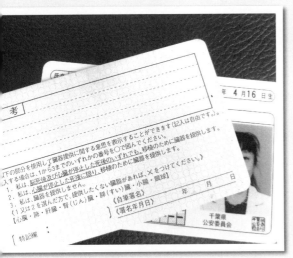

Warm-up Questions

次の質問について考えてみましょう。

1. The title of this unit suggests that few Japanese are willing to donate organs. Do you think this is true? If so, why do you think this is?

2. Do you know how to become an organ donor? What do you have to do to become an organ donor? Have you ever talked about organ donation with your family or friends?

Vocabulary Check

🔊 **Audio 43**

次の単語の意味を a 〜 j のなかから選びましょう。

1. _____ organ (*n.*)	**a.**	a piece of paper used for filling out some information
2. _____ transplant (*v.*)	**b.**	move from one person's body to another person's body
3. _____ damage (*v.*)	**c.**	parts of the body, such as the heart and kidneys, which perform important functions for life
4. _____ disease (*n.*)		
5. _____ factor (*n.*)	**d.**	a store that sells drugs or medicine
6. _____ declare (*v.*)	**e.**	reason for; one part of a situation
7. _____ form (*n.*)	**f.**	announce or make known
8. _____ municipal (*adj.*)	**g.**	decline or deny a request or demand
9. _____ pharmacy (*n.*)	**h.**	a serious illness or sickness
10. _____ refuse (*v.*)	**i.**	injure or harm
	j.	related to a city or town or local government

Pre-reading Quiz

本文を読む前に次の質問について答えましょう。

Many people in Japan are waiting for organ transplants. Which organ do you think is most needed?

a) heart **b)** liver **c)** kidneys

A businesswoman from France has just received her first Japanese driver's license. She wants to understand what is written on the back.

Imagine you were involved in a terrible car accident. Your situation was hopeless. Would you want parts of your body to be used to help someone else? Many organs can be transplanted from one body to another. At present, there are over 13,000 people in Japan on the waiting list for a donated organ because their
5 own organ has failed or has been damaged by disease or injury. The greatest need is for kidneys.

Unfortunately, very few Japanese are willing to become donors, so most of those patients will die while waiting for an organ that could save their lives. In the United States, where organ donation is better accepted, there are 7,000 to
10 8,000 organ transplants every year, or about 26 organ transplants per million people. In Japan that figure is just 0.9 transplants per million, the lowest rate in the industrialized world. On average, fewer than 100 organ transplants are performed every year in Japanese hospitals. What accounts for this low rate of donation? One factor is the traditional belief that a body should remain whole.

15 Nevertheless, opinion polls in recent years show that more people in Japan are now willing to donate. If, in the case of your death, you'd like your organs to be used to help another person, you can declare your willingness to become an organ donor by completing the form on the back of your driver's license or health-insurance card. You can also record your wishes on an organ-donation
20 decision card (*zōki teikyō ishi kādo*) that is available free at municipal offices and some pharmacies. It's a good idea to discuss your wishes with your family. Family members have the right to refuse donation, and if your wishes aren't clear, the law also allows them to make a decision in favor of donation.

✏ *300 words*

NO**T**E**S** ||||||||||||||||||||||||||||||||||||||||||||||||||||||||||||||||||||||||||||||||||||||||||||||||||||||
l. 10: transplant 移植   l. 15: opinion poll 世論調査   l. 22: have the right to ～する権利がある

Reading Comprehension: True or False

本文で述べられていることについて正しいものに T、間違っているものに F を選び○で囲みましょう。

1. (T F) A majority of Japanese are willing to become organ donors.
2. (T F) Japan has about the same rate of organ transplants as other industrialized countries.
3. (T F) Filling out the paperwork to become an organ donor is free.

Listening: Dialogue

🔊 **Audio 45**

臓器提供

次の会話を聴き、空所を埋めましょう。

Masaru and Jen are talking about the issue of organ donation.

Masaru: Can I ask you something? What does this mean on your ① _____ _____?

Jen: Oh, that? That just means I'm an ② _____ _____.

Masaru: Oh, so if you die in a ③ _____ _____ or something you'll donate your organs?

Jen: That's right. ④ _____ _____ _____ the same information on your license?

Masaru: No, I don't. Actually, I didn't ⑤ _____ _____ about such a system.

Jen: But you ⑥ _____ _____ organ donors in Japan too, right?

Masaru: Well, we do have them, but I think the number of donors is ⑦ _____ _____.

Jen: That's a shame. If you agree to donate your organs, you might ⑧ _____ someone's ⑨ _____ someday.

Masaru: Yeah, I guess I should ⑩ _____ _____ it more. So almost everyone in your country is an organ donor?

Jen: Well, most people support organ donation, but ⑪ _____ _____ _____ have actually registered to become organ donors!

True or False

もう一度会話を聴き、正しいものに T を、間違っているものに F を○で囲みましょう。

1. (T F) Masaru and Jen have the same information on their driver's license.
2. (T F) There are some organ donors in Japan too.
3. (T F) Almost everyone in Jen's country is a registered organ donor.

Grammar Check

会話に出てきた表現を確認しながら（　　　）内の適切な語を選びましょう。

1. This sign (ⓐ mean ⓑ means) you can't park your car here.
2. (ⓐ Aren't ⓑ Don't) you feel cold? Let's turn on the heater.
3. There is just a small (ⓐ number   ⓑ numbers) of organ transplants in Japan every year.
4. (ⓐ Almost ⓑ Most) Japanese people eat rice every day.

パートナーと次のトピックについて話し合ってみましょう。

1. Would you like to become an organ donor? Why or why not? Explain your reasons.

2. Imagine you are seriously ill. The only way you can live is to receive a donated organ. You would have part of another person transplanted into your body. Would you agree to this? Why or why not?

▶ **Topic Expansion**

Look at the diagram below. Match each organ of the body with its name in English, writing the correct number in the blank.

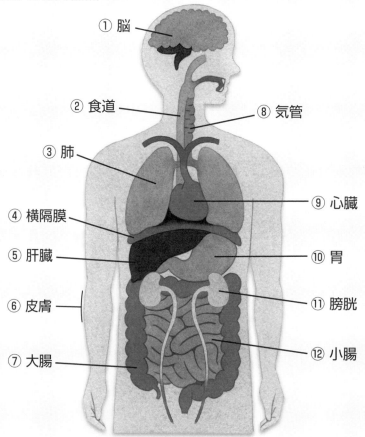

① 脳
② 食道
③ 肺
④ 横隔膜
⑤ 肝臓
⑥ 皮膚
⑦ 大腸
⑧ 気管
⑨ 心臓
⑩ 胃
⑪ 膀胱
⑫ 小腸

brain _____	diaphragm _____	esophagus _____	heart _____
kidneys _____	large intestine _____	liver _____	lungs _____
skin _____	small intestine _____	stomach _____	trachea _____

▼写真出典

《表紙》（右上）© よっちゃん必撮仕事人 / PIXTA（ピクスタ）
　　　　（左下）© kuro3 / PIXTA（ピクスタ）
　　　　（右下）© horiphoto / PIXTA（ピクスタ）

《本文》p. 3 © Alice Gordenker ／ p. 7 © Alice Gordenker ／ p. 11 © とんとん / PIXTA（ピクスタ）／ p. 15 © H.Kuwagaki / PIXTA（ピクスタ）／ p. 23 © 八王子市 ／ p. 27 © Skylight / PIXTA（ピクスタ）／ p. 31 © Alice Gordenker ／ p. 35 © blanche/ PIXTA（ピクスタ）／ p. 43 © Alice Gordenker ／ p. 47 © foly/ PIXTA（ピクスタ）／ p. 51 © jazzman/ PIXTA（ピクスタ）／ p. 55 © Alice Gordenker ／ p. 59 © Alice Gordenker

▼画像・挿絵

《本文》p. 14 © hanako/ PIXTA（ピクスタ）／ p. 62 うえむらのぶこ

Surprising Japan! 2
ニッポンの不思議 2

2023 年 4 月 10 日　初版第 1 刷発行

著　　者　Alice Gordenker ／ John Rucynski

発 行 者　森　信久
発 行 所　株式会社　松 柏 社
　　　　　〒102-0072　東京都千代田区飯田橋 1-6-1
　　　　　TEL　03 (3230) 4813（代表）
　　　　　FAX　03 (3230) 4857
　　　　　http://www.shohakusha.com
　　　　　e-mail: info@shohakusha.com

装　　幀　　小島トシノブ（NONdesign）
本文レイアウト　　一柳　茂（株式会社クリエーターズユニオン）
組　　版　　木野内宏行（ALIUS）
印刷・製本　　シナノ書籍印刷株式会社

ISBN978-4-88198-780-3
略号＝ 780
Copyright © 2023 Alice Gordenker & John Rucynski